Millennium
Mom

Millennium
Mom

tips and time savers to go from a
working woman to a working mom

by Joanna Zucker

Published by Clerisy Press
Printed in the United States of America
Distributed by Publishers Group West
First edition, first printing

For further information, contact the publisher at:

CLERISY PRESS

Clerisy Press
1700 Madison Road
Cincinnati, OH 45206
www.clerisypress.com

Library of Congress Cataloging-in-Publication Data:

Zucker, Joanna.
Millennium mom : 100 tips and time savers to go from a working woman
to a working mom / by Joanna Zucker. -- 1st ed.
    p. cm.
 ISBN-13: 978-1-57860-336-7
 ISBN-10: 1-57860-336-6
 1. Working mothers--Life skills guides. 2. Work and family. 3.
Mothers--Life skills guides. I. Title.

HQ759.48.Z83 2008
646.70085'2--dc22
                                        2008036588
Cover designed by Stephen Sullivan
Cover photo by John Walters
Interior and production design by Donna Collingwood
Photos by John Walters

*T*his book is dedicated to my parents, John and Mary Ann Prokosch. They have been married for forty-two years! They encouraged each of their children to work hard and follow their dreams, despite only holding high-school degrees themselves. They never missed an event, allowed me to make my own decisions, and cushioned my falls when they were the wrong ones. I am what I am today as a businessperson, wife, mother, friend, and person because of their example. Thank you very much, and I love you more than words can say.

Acknowledgments

I could not have written this book without a lot of love and encouragement. First and foremost from my husband, who made me believe that I could do this and encouraged me to do so even when I thought I couldn't. Thanks for dangling that carrot in front of me. To my parents, without their glowing example of how to be great parents, I couldn't be where I am today. To my baby group: Kristi Leonard, Jacqueline Denham, Nina Urban, and Kristen Illingworth for reading my first draft and providing invaluable advice and builds. To Kristine Decker, Karen Hoffman, Marie Mound, Lynanne Kunkel, Heather Chambers, Jill Cavanagh, Louisa Shields, Kristen Mortinez, and Karen Powers for their thorough reviews and feedback. To Gerald Bagg for igniting the spark in me through his encouraging words and ideas. Finally to my children who make it all worthwhile each and every day, my world is complete with all of you in it.

Author's Note

I provide a lot of tips throughout this book, many of which refer to specific products that I use. Please note that all of these recommendations are based on my use and experience with the products and are unsolicited, including products by Procter & Gamble.

Table of Contents

Introduction

As I sit down with my laptop to begin writing "my book," I am eight-and-a-half months pregnant with my third child. My goal for this maternity leave, eight months in length, is to not only welcome our new addition, shower it with love and nurture him or her into a healthy infant, but also to tackle many home projects and to finally write the book I have dreamed of. The inspiration behind this book is threefold. First, after delivering my first baby, Ben, I took ten months maternity leave. While on leave I read quite a bit and saw quite a few good reviews and articles regarding the book *I Don't Know How She Does It* by British author Allison Pearson. The book was hailed as "a sparkling novel about juggling marriage, kids, and job (and getting some sleep)." Because I was about to start juggling marriage, kids, and a job, I was excited to read this book and had high expectations for it. At the time I was a brand manager for Procter & Gamble, the world's largest consumer-product company. I had been with P&G for five years and had just finished my first brand-manager assignment which happened to be an ex-patriate assignment in Belgium. My husband, Arnie, also worked for P&G in finance and accounting. We both had MBAs—mine from the University of Michigan and Arnie's from Duke University—and loved our jobs. I was looking for some tips and thought the novel could give them to me. While I knew it was fiction, I was still hopeful I might learn a few things as I prepared to re-enter the workplace upon our return to the U.S. My birthday was approaching so when asked by my mother-in-law what I wanted, I mentioned the book and couldn't wait to start reading it. While the book was humorous—and, in hindsight, after having kids, very realistic at times—it did not offer a lot of insight into how to best manage your busy life as a working mom. In fact the key take-away from the book would be that it is almost impossible to manage it all. When I finished the book all I could think of was "please don't let this be me." I want to have it all—a successful career, loving marriage, and terrific family. So, in June 2003 we moved back to the U.S., and I returned to work nervous but hopeful that we could manage it all: our two careers, our beautiful son, our new home in the suburbs (that was a big adjustment), and our marriage, which so far was the highlight of my life.

Our move back to Cincinnati went relatively smoothly. Our belongings arrived before we did so we could move in right after we closed on the house. Ben was registered and settling into Procter & Gamble's daycare, which allowed me time to do some painting and organizing during my last two weeks off before I began work. In general, my re-entry into work went well. I took on a two-month special assignment that allowed a lot of flexibility in my workday. This was a blessing as Arnie was busier than ever. So things were going really well when God decided to throw us for a bit of a loop—I got pregnant. You can all laugh to yourselves and wonder how we could be surprised by this. I agree, we were thirty-three and thirty-seven years old, had already conceived one child, and were pretty educated on the birds and the bees. We had also been forewarned by a few of our friends about how fertile you are when you stop breast-feeding, something I had done about six weeks beforehand. But none of this came to mind or seemed to matter when the news arrived.

My new assignment as the Bounce brand manager began September 1. I was working for a manager I had worked for before, and we had a strong personal relationship. This eased my fears a bit, but they all came back when four of my colleagues, who were also brand managers in my business unit, announced they were expecting prior to me notifying my manager. In due time I told my boss and he was thrilled for me and supportive of my decision to take four months' leave and return to the same role. So at this point I was settling into my assignment, readjusting to being back in Cincinnati and in the suburbs for the first time, pregnant with my second child, and still cherishing my marriage to Arnie and the joy of my first child—but winging it when it came to managing all of it together.

This brings me to the second inspiration for this book, my mother-in-law Marsha Zucker (who bought me my first inspiration). Throughout my pregnancy, as we remodeled, settled in, took vacations, and I continued to work at P&G, her constant question to me was, "How do you do it?" My life was very different from hers. She had been a stay-at-home mom to Arnie and his brother, so she never dealt with daycare, a fifty-plus-hour workweek, and the crazed modern lives we all live, so I could understand how it would seem foreign to her. But she truly wondered how Arnie and I made it all work. Ben was a great kid who was well-adjusted and generally happy. Arnie and I had a great marriage filled with love, respect, and fun. Our home was a happy place that was well managed and genuinely neat most of the time with the exception of a few toys lying around here and there.

Ironically, my in-laws were visiting us for the weekend (thankfully) when Claire decided to come into the world two-and-a-half weeks early. Given that I was supposed to work for three more days, there were meetings to cancel, etc. This was all happening while Ben's big-boy furniture was being delivered and installed. Through all this my mother-in-law quietly and nervously stood by watching and encouraging Arnie and me to go to the hospital. She again said to me, "I really don't know how you do it." At that moment I began to ask myself the same question…how do we do it? How do we manage our life in a way that rewards us, makes us happy, feel balanced, and fulfills us. I tried to answer all of these questions while on my four-month leave with Claire. I decided to write down all the things that I did on a daily, weekly, or monthly basis that helped us keep things organized and saved us time. I guess you could say my research was done while on leave with Claire.

I began to talk to people about my idea and most people thought it was a good one, but one person in particular gave me my third inspiration: Gerald Bagg, CEO of Quigley Simpson, my Direct Response Television agency located in L.A. Gerald is a wonderful man with an incredible amount of industry and life experience. I always enjoyed his visits to Cincinnati to chat about the world, our industry, pop culture, or any other interesting topic. In one of our team meetings, we were talking about the Bounce target consumer, and we called her "the simplicity seeker." The joke on our team was that I was she in many ways, hence I was asked to critique our ideas and plans as if I were the consumer. This led our agency to pick my brain for timesaving tips or ingenious shortcuts that I used to manage my household. When I shared some of these with Gerald he told me he thought I was on to something and that there was probably an audience for my ideas and my book. Whether because I had such respect for him, or whether he offered to read it and help me, either way this was enough inspiration for me to decide I would set the goal of writing my book when on leave with my third child.

So, here I am today, waiting for baby Zucker Number Three to arrive and sitting down to put my ideas and tips on paper. I am thrilled to tackle this challenge and scared to death at the same time. I am a marketer by education and training. I know how to do it and do it well. I have an incredible support network both inside and outside of work, but have no idea how to write a book. Am I nuts? Probably so, but I am also hopeful that perhaps I can help people like Arnie and me—busy people who strive to have it all, but at the same time realize it is difficult to have it all. If I can save households time, allowing parents to spend more time with their kids, or help women set better expectations so they can feel that they succeed every now and then, it will all be worth it. I hope you enjoy this simple book of tips, and ideas that may allow you to feel like you know how to manage it all and, at times, actually feel like you have succeeded.

The content of the book is divided into two main sections: 1) cardinal rules, and 2) tips and time savers. My original thoughts for the book were the tips and time savers. But when I thought about my tips for each area of life, I began to realize that even with the tips, managing a household with two careers and children would be very difficult without certain factors. I also talked to a lot of people and realized that, regardless of how organized they were, many were still not successfully managing work, family, and themselves. When I probed further, the reasons typically fell into four main areas, which I developed into my cardinal rules. You at least need to be aware of these rules and try to improve them to make life a bit easier for everyone. When you read the cardinal rules ask yourself if you can honestly answer yes to each of the questions—

- Is managing the house and kids a partnership?
- Did you choose the right career and, ideally, the right employer to have it all?
- Are you completely satisfied with your childcare?
- Do you have a goal you are working towards?

If you can't say yes to all of these, it's okay. While it may be difficult, it is never too late to make a career switch, change daycare providers, or establish a goal. It is also never too late to try to get your husband or partner to do more around the house. Later I will provide you with some key discussion starters and questions to ask to guide you as you make decisions or try to get a little more help around the home and with the kids. Whatever change you decide to make, use this book as a guide to help navigate through those changes.

The tips and time savers are divided into five areas: household, children, you, career, and life. I believe they are self explanatory with one exception. What is the difference between the household and life? The household tips revolve around saving time and energy in household tasks and the running of the household. Tips for managing life include all those things that happen in life and take time to plan and organize like vacations, birthdays, entertaining, photo albums, and more. You'll find symbols to help you understand what each tip gives you. Look for the symbol next to each tip.

tips that will save you time

tips that will save you stress

tips that will make you happy

I hope you benefit from reading this book and that your life becomes a little better as a result. While not all the tips may be applicable to your current situation, you will find at least some of them helpful and life changing in some way, and you can refer back to others at another time.

The Cardinal Rules

It Takes a Partnership

*M*anaging a career and children takes a lot of work, typically more than one person can handle. To find happiness and satisfaction with this lifestyle you need a true partnership with your partner when it comes to running the house. For the single parents who don't have a partner in the home, I have the highest admiration for you because you face challenges most married couples would not know how to handle. My hope is that my tips will also help you save valuable time and energy through shortcuts and solutions that will make your life easier overall.

For those of you who are married but don't yet have a true partnership, it is not too late. While we are over a half-century beyond the June Cleaver 1950s, many men have not evolved very far when it comes to managing the household. While I love my dad to death, he will be the first to admit that the first diaper he changed was his granddaughter's, and that most household duties like cleaning are still my mom's. With my career, this arrangement would be impossible. In fact, anything less than 50/50 would tip the scale enough that my life would be chaotic compared to the nice rhythm it has today.

Take the time to sit down with your partner and talk about what you need help with. Here is what I recommend:

1. Sit down before the baby arrives (or right now if you have kids) and talk about the changes in the household and how you are going to manage them (feeding baby, changing baby, dressing baby, bathing baby, dropping off/ picking up baby).

2. Reassess your current roles in the home (laundry, cooking, cleaning, yard maintenance, etc.). The responsibilities probably will have to change as your available time has changed now that the baby needs to be cared for. Perhaps you can outsource more or switch roles to better accommodate your new schedule.

3. Be honest with your partner. If you are stressed, explain what is causing the stress. I truly believe most men are clueless when it comes to what causes their wives to lose their minds sometimes. Your assumption should be "he simply doesn't know I am so busy that I can't think and that he needs to help me" when you start your conversation with him. I will get into specific tasks and processes to help you manage the house and kids, but the key is having a partner to help get it all done.

I had always thought my husband Arnie was a pretty good partner, but when I sat down to write this book I thought it would be a good idea to look up the official definition to see how our partnership measured up. Webster's dictionary definition is:

> **part•ner** (pärt'nər) *noun* 1. a person who takes part in some activity in common with another or others: associate; specif., a) one of two or more persons engaged in the same business enterprise and sharing its profits and risks: each is an agent for the other or others and is liable, except when limited to his own investment, for the debts of the firm, b) a husband or wife, c) either of two persons dancing together, d) either of two players on the same side or team playing or competing against two others, as in bridge or tennis.

Our family and household is very much like running a business. Our profit is the unconditional love we get from each other and our children; our risks are financial, spiritual, and emotional in nature. We are both liable for the decisions we make and their short- and long-term impact on our household and our family. Our daily ritual is like a modern dance. We use fancy footwork each morning to get the family out the door and each evening as we prepare our dinner, bathe the kids, and go through our bedtime routine. We are husband and wife, but also teammates, finishing each other's work, complementing each others strengths and weaknesses, all in an effort to win in life.

I know I am lucky in life to have found a man like Arnie, and that not all women are so fortunate. But, he also took a lot of work ☺. It is never too late to talk to your husband and work together to form a better partnership. You fell in love with (and have chosen to have a family with) this person. You have faith and trust in him. Use that as the foundation to build your partnership. Take time away from the house to sit down and have an adult conversation. Let him know where you are struggling and what help you need. Start with a few areas where he can help, and once he masters those, add some more.

To summarize, if having a career and family is your goal, make sure to share this goal with your partner. If you didn't have this discussion before marriage, it is important to have it before or right after you have children. Ask yourselves how you will work together to manage it all, and go through my recommended tips to help guide this discussion and decision making. If you have had children and are struggling to manage it all, start with the division of tasks worksheet in appendix E to help divide the housework to reduce some of your stress. Also, don't be afraid to have your husband read the tips in this book. They are simple and easy to follow and will help the entire household run more smoothly.

Choose the Right Career and Employer

While not as life-altering as the choice of a life mate, the choice of a profession can also play a significant role in your ability to manage a career with kids. Let's talk about the reality of your career. Unless you are fortunate to find a fulfilling part-time position in your field, which is difficult to do, at a minimum you will spend thirty-five to forty hours each week at your job. If you fall into the category of full-time in a salaried position, this is more likely to be more than fifty hours per week. That's average. There are plenty of careers that demand more time, which is why choosing the right career is so important.

When deciding on a career or job, the first thing you should think about is what you love to do. What makes you happy? What are your personal passions? Ideally, you can find a job that allows you to do what you love. If you can't find a job doing something you love, then I recommend finding one you are good at. If you are going to spend forty plus hours a week doing it, either love it or be good at it; otherwise you will be miserable and your household will be too. Helpful tools when trying to find a job are books or counselors that can help you identify jobs that fit your skills or passions. The key is to share your passions and strengths so they know what to work from.

I made one of the biggest mistakes in my life by allowing a guidance counselor to talk me into something that was not a fit for me. When I graduated in 1992 with a B.S. in marketing, the economy was very weak and marketing jobs were few and far between. Looking at my grades and strengths, a counselor suggested I apply to law school. It was a great degree to have, you didn't need work experience, and I could always go into business after graduation. Before I knew it, I had taken the LSAT, applied to a variety of schools, and enrolled in Emory University's School of Law. Not until I was sitting in orientation did I ever ask myself…is this really what I want to do? Luckily, I had the strength and self-confidence to admit it wasn't and convinced my parents I had made a huge mistake. I withdrew and have never looked back. The moral of the story is to follow your passions instead of taking the easy way out.

If you like to turn to books for help, some well-known titles are *What Color is Your Parachute?; I Don't Know What I Want, But I Know It's Not This; The Pathfinder;* and *Do What You Are.* The premise behind each of these books is to identify what you like and what innate skills you have, and then match these with a career. It is never too late to turn to books like these. Often you don't discover your inert strengths and skills until later in life, since they can develop over time.

When you find a field you like or have multiple jobs to choose from, quickly go over the pros and cons of each option. Here are some things to consider as they will affect your ability to manage it all down the road:

- Location—Where are the jobs located? What is the cost-of-living index for each location? What is the average commute time in each city? How close to family is each job? For example, after graduating from business school I didn't want to return to the high cost of living on the East Coast and wouldn't move to the West Coast because it was too far from family, and so I focused on the Midwest.

- Travel—How much travel is required? Is it domestic or international? Short or long trips?

■ Work Hours—What is the average workweek like? Is there any flexibility in the hours? For example, can you leave to attend your child's T-ball game?

■ Security—If job security is important to you, as well as long-term security, you may want to look at larger, well-established companies versus smaller firms, start-ups, or self-employment. Ask yourself how much risk do you want to take.

Some things that were not on my list, but perhaps could be on yours are:

■ Salary

■ Benefits—Health, vacation, signing bonus, stock options, bonuses

■ Speed of Advancement—How quick to promotion?

■ Equity stake

While this list will help you identify careers that are appealing to you and make getting out of bed and leaving your kids each day easier, it won't help you identify careers that work better for busy households. I would encourage you to be wary of jobs that require either a lot of hours (more than fifty-five hours per week) or have irregular hours, such as consulting, investment banking, doctors who are constantly on call, a pilot or flight attendant. While they may be very rewarding jobs, they will put additional stress on the household due to the increased time away from home. Jobs that require frequent travel or overnight trips make childcare difficult, but can be managed if you have the help of family or friends.

Likewise, there are jobs that lend themselves to managing your career and kids because they have similar schedules to schools and/or have more flexible hours. For example, school teachers have a day off every day their children do (for the most part); banking and government jobs share all major holidays with children; and real estate allows you to work on evenings and weekends (the opposite of a partner perhaps), which may limit the amount of childcare you need.

After you find a career you love or are good at, you will, ideally, find it with the right employer. Two job descriptions may look identical on paper, but can turn out to be very different once you are in the role. The culture within a company, government, or school district impacts every employee through the beliefs, values, and principles by which it operates. Its benefits impact your family deeply with regard to vacation time, healthcare, maternity leave, retirement plans, and more. Follow your gut when you are trying to decide which school district, company, or employer to work for. Personal fit is very important and will have a huge impact on your happiness over time.

If you are choosing a job or ever decide to leave your current job for another, the first thing you should do is talk to current employees of the company. Before interviewing, try to locate alumni from your school who work for the firm and talk to them. With the Internet and alumni networks, it is very easy to find people—they are your best resource, and you should utilize them. If you are switching jobs to another local firm, check with neighbors and family to see if they know anyone at the employer you are interviewing with or interested in joining. If you don't find any alumni, consider asking these questions in your interview when you are given the opportunity.

- How long is the average workday?
- How much travel is required for the position?
- What are the career paths or options within the company?
- What is the culture of the company? (Does it appear to you to be competitive or supportive?)
- Have you ever had to compromise your personal values or morals for the company?
- Are there women in management? What percentage of the management team is female?
- Do you know any women in a dual-career marriage who also have children?

- What do you like least about your company?

I can't encourage you enough to find a company that fits your personal values. There are many things that happen in life that will cause you to need a break from work, a more flexible schedule or a longer leave of absence, like a sick family member or your own health. It is important to know that your company will support you through these times with whatever you need. While I was in Europe my younger brother was diagnosed with cancer. My boss and entire team supported me during this very tough time and gave me the flexibility I needed. This allowed me to travel to New York to be with my brother and work remotely from there. I have found values drive how companies operate, so find out what the driving principles are before you join an organization.

In the end, you want to "interview" and conduct a background check on the company you are interviewing with. What are its benefits, culture and philosophy regarding key life elements that will have a huge affect on your physical and mental well-being? It will become very apparent what companies rise to the top of your list—and what companies you can't run away from fast enough.

Choose Childcare Wisely

*M*anaging a dual-career household is not difficult. In fact it can be quite simple given that you have two incomes versus one income. This above-average disposable income allows you to manage your busy life via "outsourcing"—like eating out and hiring help for many household tasks (cleaning the home, maintaining the yard, dry cleaning pickup/dropoff, painting, grocery shopping, etc.). Managing a dual-career household *with children* is a whole different ballgame. Children bring great joy to life and a home, more than words can ever express. They also bring chaos into life with their demands and needs. If you are working eight-plus hours a day, you are not physically present to manage your kids' needs; hence, you must find someone else to do it for you while you work Monday through Friday. This brings me to the toughest decision you will make post-delivery of your child: who will care for your child?

Thankfully, with so many households with both parents working there are more choices than ever regarding the care of your children. While not all of these may be applicable to your home due to budget constraints, it is important to understand the range of choices for future reference and to compare and contrast in the cases where cost is not an issue. Most choices fall into four areas:

1. Nanny/au pair childcare in your home

2. Small-scale in-home daycare in someone else's home

3. Larger-scale daycare center (including company-provided as they are usually larger in size)

4. Family member

Each of these options has its pros and cons, which I will attempt to illustrate below; however, more important than the pros and cons is what option best fits your needs and wishes for your children and feels right to you. As each child is unique, each parent is also unique, and you must choose the option that feels the most comfortable for you and your child.

Nanny

Pros

- Personal attention for your children
- Ability to drive children to activities, preschool, etc.
- In-home, so no need to get children ready during hectic morning hours
- May do some household tasks for you, such as laundry or cooking
- Long-term provider for your child (no change in classroom or teacher)
- No worries about curriculum (you can set it)
- Limited exposure to germs
- Do not have to cover child's sick days
- No need to change care provider when one child turns to school age

Cons

- Expensive—anywhere from $20,000-50,000 per year or more, depending on how your pay (cash or not) and number of children
- Limited interaction with other children/persons
- Limited hours (Most work no more than ten hours per day. You need to include your commute time, so limits hours you can work outside the home.)
- Trust—you need to have an incredible amount of trust in the nanny as they are in your home and alone with your children
- May need to provide a suitably sized vehicle for the nanny to use
- Need to have a backup plan for nanny's vacation and sick days

Au Pair

An au pair is a nanny that lives in your house. Often the au pair is foreign and younger than many domestic nannies, usually nineteen to twenty-four years old, and only stays one year. There are many organizations that place au pairs in U.S. homes for a fee, so you do have someone to turn to if any issues should arise.

Pros
- Personal attention for your children
- Ability to drive children to activities, preschool, etc.
- In-home, so no need to get children ready during hectic morning hours
- May do some household tasks for you, like laundry or cooking
- No worries about curriculum (you can set it)
- Limited exposure to germs
- Do not have to cover child's sick days
- Children's exposure to another culture
- Flexibility–you can determine the hours you want and often au pair can cover evenings or weekends for additional cost
- Cost–cheaper than a nanny as they receive room and board, often about $15,000 per year

Cons
- Young age can mean limited-to-no experience with young children
- Limited interaction with other children/persons
- Meals–you need to shop for food to feed children during the day
- Trust–you need to have an incredible amount of trust in the au pair as they become a member of your household while they live with you

- A nonfamily member living in your household (noise, habits, mess, etc.)
- Must have room for au pair in the house
- Contract often requires a car for au pair to use
- Typically do not stay with a family for more than a year despite children's attachment

Small-scale In-home Daycare

Pros

- Small size; usually only two to eight children, depending on state laws (be sure to check for certification documents when visiting)
- Meals are sometimes covered in contract
- Reasonable price ($500-$1,200 per month, price varies by where you live)
- Interaction with other children
- Often close to your home
- Flexible hours (often work with parents' needs, including having older children dropped off after school, etc.)
- Personal—often referred by family or friends

Cons

- Children exposed to other children's germs
- Must cover days when child is sick
- Limited curriculum—often less qualified than nannies, au pairs, and staff at daycare centers with regards to early childhood care
- Children's ages are often across a broad range (from infant to preschool)
- Trust—while there are other children around, usually the only adult with your child is the care provider
- Less personal attention
- Less control of what goes on in someone else's home, e.g., too much TV
- At the mercy of the provider's vacation schedule
- Young children can be exposed to the habits of older children

Daycare Center

Pros

- Extended hours (ranges depending on location, but often 7 a.m.-6 p.m.)
- Must meet state requirements regarding child:teacher ratio, health codes, safety certification (be sure to check for documents)
- Highly qualified staff
- Meals are often provided
- Interaction with other children
- Flexibility—often has numerous classrooms if one does not meet your needs
- Reasonable price (about $500-1,100 per month, per child) Premium-cost centers typically have more experienced care providers and longer hours, but often have higher turnover rates among providers
- Children are in classroom with age-alike children
- Curriculum—most offer many activities for children

Cons

- Exposure to other children's germs
- Must cover sick days
- Some do not cover meals
- Often doesn't work once oldest child reaches school age (due to different schedule and location)
- Larger scale may be intimidating or lack personal feel
- Less personal attention
- Logistics of dropoff and pickup times, no flexibility, and can incur late fee

Family Member

Pros

- Familiar to your children
- High level of trust
- Lower cost (usually cheaper than small daycare, $250-750 per month)
- Meals are usually provided
- Your children can be together
- Flexibility—if you need to work late, travel, or child is sick
- Limited exposure to germs
- Do not have to cover child's sick days
- Personal attention for your children
- Ability to drive children to activities, preschool, etc.
- Long-term provider for your children (no change in classroom or teacher)

Cons

- It's family—hard to discipline their philosophy on childcare
- Usually in their home, so morning still hectic
- Limited interaction with other children/persons
- May not be trained childcare provider
- May not get as much exposure to curriculum as with other providers

I am sure I will receive many letters and e-mails highlighting pros and cons that I have missed (for the record, I would welcome them), as I have only had personal exposure to one of these options. Additionally, you may have other pros and cons based on your personal situation. For example, you have a special-needs child, and one of the options may be better than others in an area that is extremely important to you. This is why you need to think about what you want for your child, what you can afford, and make the decision for your family. I can only encourage you to look at all the options and take the decision very seriously as it will affect your life more than you can imagine—either in a positive or negative way, depending on how it turns out.

Once you make your choice, remember that no decision is final. If at any time you are losing sleep thinking about the care of your child, re-evaluate your situation/decision and make a change if necessary. For example, friends of ours had their child in a day-care center but he was out sick more than he was at the center. This forced them to spend an incredible amount of money on last-minute babysitter services that charge $10-30 per hour (again, based on where you live) due to the urgent need. When they added it up they might as well have a nanny because it would be cheaper, and they would have less stress worrying about who would cover the sick days. They switched to a nanny and have never looked back as it was the perfect situation for them and significantly cut back on their child's illnesses. Evaluate your childcare situation on a regular basis to ensure it continues to be the best option. Like many things in life— what works now may not work tomorrow or in the future.

Additionally, what works today may not work in a few years. As I make final edits to this book (in March 2008) before it goes to print, we are preparing to transition our care provider. We have had almost five amazing years at Children for Children's daycare. We could not have been happier with the care our children received and their development. But situations change. Ben will be going to kindergarten in the fall, which changes our needs. Our school district only has half-day kindergarten, which means Ben needs to be on the bus at 8:45 A.M. and will get home at noon. We can get him before-school care at the school, and arrange for a local daycare to pick him up from school, but that would mean three different care providers for him throughout the day. We felt that was a lot for a six-year-old. After weighing all our options, we have decided to move to a nanny this summer. The nanny will get Ben onto the bus, watch the girls all day, and be home to get Ben off the bus. This is also the best long-term solution as next year Ben will be full-day and Claire will only be half-day. Even if we had figured out next year, we would again be in a pinch the year after that. We are sad about leaving Children for Children, but have faith we will find an amazing nanny who will shower our children with love and kindness, and make our days a bit simpler as we transition to our "school years."

Have an End Goal You Are Working Toward

*L*eaving your children each day is not an easy thing to do, and I would be remiss if I did not tell you there will be guilt associated with it. You will ask yourself many times as you leave your children each day, "Why am I doing this?" You want to be sure you know the answer to this question.

Given the incredible success of *Desperate Housewives*, we are all a little more aware of the stress and guilt associated with being a working mom (thanks, Lynette!). But even Lynette's situation is better than the average American, as her husband is home with the children. Most Americans are not fortunate enough to have a family member or friend care for their children each day (though their care providers will feel like family quickly). So why do so many women work and leave their kids each day only to feel guilt? The answers vary greatly, but ideally share one common quality…because the moms are working toward a goal that makes the sacrifice and guilt worth it. For most women the goal is to provide the best home and lifestyle for their family; it is a financial decision. But this is not always the case and even when it is, there are some key things to keep in mind to help guide you.

The most crucial thing a dual-career couple has to remember is *you should not live at or beyond your means*. Let me explain a bit.

Despite the fact that the majority of households in the U.S. earn two incomes, about 70 percent of them live paycheck to paycheck. Further, there is more debt in America now than ever before. What is causing this financial crisis in the U.S.? It certainly wasn't this way when our parents' generation raised their families. Most of our moms didn't work and yet they raised happy and healthy families, often larger in size than today. How did our parents do it? Why didn't they rack up debt like households today? The answer is simple: They didn't live beyond their means. In many households there were strict budgets, and they worked very hard to stay within them. On the flip side, today most households live beyond their means by spending all that they make (and often more). More income just means more "stuff"…a larger house, a more expensive car, more toys, more gadgets, more vacations, a second home, a boat, you name it. Unfortunately, most of the time it doesn't mean more savings, more college funds for the children, or more security if something should happen. Americans often live beyond their means; if they have it, they spend it and often spend more than they have. This is why it is important to have a goal. This will help drive your financial choices and purchase decisions each month. Without a goal you will feel trapped by your job and often end up hating your work. Here are some examples of goals you might have:

- To be able to pay for your children's college education
- To be able to retire at a certain age (and usually this means early)
- To be able to stay home at some point
- To pay off debt so you can eventually survive on one income
- To achieve a certain level of success in your career

There is one common element in most of the goals described above: they require saving money. Hence, despite having two incomes, you are not "living" off two incomes because a portion of the income is going into savings or being invested. This is why you should live below your means despite the temptation to spend what you make. Reframe your thinking to "what do I *need* versus what do I *want*." Sit down with your spouse and figure out a rough budget to give yourself some guidance as to what you could potentially save each year towards your goal. I have outlined a very simple budget template below for reference. There are many online tools as well if you would like more detailed spreadsheets (like Quicken).

Example of Household Budget

 | ***Income*** |
 | **Less Taxes** |
= | **Net Income** |

- Fixed/Monthly expenses like:
-    Housing Expense (mortgage/rent, property taxes if you own)
-    Utilities (gas & electric, phone, cable, water, garbage)
-    Car payments
-    Student loans
-    Insurance
-    Cell phone service
-    Childcare
-    Groceries
-    Gasoline/train card/tolls/parking

= **Net Income less fixed expenses**

- **Annual Savings Goal**

= **Income left for flexible spending**

- ***Flexible expenses***
-    Babysitting
-    Lawn service/maid
-    Entertainment (eating out, memberships, magazine subscriptions, concerts, shows, movies)
-    Kids stuff (photos, toys)
-    Clothes
-    Gifts (weddings, anniversaries, Christmas, new babies, birthdays)
-    Vacations

= **$0**

The key to any budget is to control the flexible items. I am always surprised how much our household spends each month on "nonessential" items like getting the car washed, CDs/DVDs/iTunes, or going to the circus with the kids. The way to limit the nonessential spending is to figure out how much you want to save and make choices with your spouse if your initial go-round with your budget doesn't provide enough savings. Ask yourselves what items you are willing to sacrifice to meet your goal. What can you do without? Our goal is to retire "early" so we can be with our children in their teen years. We try to save as much of my salary as possible so we can reach this goal. With this in mind we bought a house that was right for our family, but cost well below what the average family with our income pays for a house. We own our cars outright and keep them longer than the average household. We don't buy the latest gadgets as soon as they come out. We live below our means, because the long-term goal is much more important than short-term material items to us.

I encourage each of you reading this book to have a long, hard discussion regarding your household goals. Ask yourselves why you are working so hard. What is the light at the end of the tunnel? I also encourage you to break down your monthly spending and determine what areas could be cut in the case that you are not saving enough. This is really important because although you may love your job today and not want to be a stay-at-home mom, this could change in the future. And if it does, you shouldn't have to sell your house or do something drastic to make financial ends meet.

In summary, as you prepare to expand your family and continue in your career, ask yourself:

- Do I have a real partnership in life?
    - Are my husband and I clear on our responsibilities in the home, with the kids, with our outside-the-home activities, etc.? Sit down and go over my exercise in appendix E to help with this.

- Can I have it all with my current job requirements?
  - While you may want to continue to work, your current job may not be the right one to try to "manage it all" in. Think about what you are good at and what types of jobs would allow you to use those skills and strengths, but also allow you to raise a beautiful family.

- Have I found childcare I *love*?
  - Do I have 100 percent confidence in the care? Does it fit in our budget? Have I looked at all the options and found one that works for our family?

- What is my goal?
  - What goal am I trying to achieve? My family's goal? How am I going to get out of bed every day and leave my children? What is it all for?

Disclaimer on my tips

The following pages contain tips on how to manage the various aspects of your life. The tips are either from personal experience or things I have learned from family and friends. When applicable, I will recommend a specific product if I have been pleased with its performance. This does not mean that other products are not as good—simply that I have used it and was very happy with the end result. I do mention a lot of brands by name. I work in brand management and have a lot of respect for brand-building, hence I want to give credit to a specific brand versus category if that is what I have used. They have built equity with me, and I want to give them credit. I also mention quite a few Procter & Gamble brands. Given that my husband and I both work at P&G, as you would imagine, we use quite a few of their products and, in general, we are pleased with them.

I would love to hear what tips you have for a new working mother on how to make her life a bit easier. Please e-mail me the tips you would give to a friend as she makes the transition to a working mom to joanna@millenniummom.com. You can also blog with me at www.milleniummom.com. If you have any specific products or services that you use and have been happy with, I would love to hear about those as well.

Tips and Time Savers:

For Managing the Household

When you bring children into your life, nothing changes more than your house. It will transition from a *house* to a *home*. It will go from a *house* to a *household*. It won't smell the same, look the same, feel the same, or be as clean as it was before you had kids. The level of activity will multiply and whole rooms will be taken over by toys and baby stuff. Given all this change that is happening it is crucial that you have tips to help you manage the home. The following tips will help you keep your home somewhat clean, organized, and running smoothly.

Before the tips there are two "top ten lists" for you. The first is my "if money were not an issue, the top ten things I would recommend in your home" to make life a bit easier to manage. Some of these are related to the kids, others organization and household tasks. As I thought about the features of my home that really help make my life easier, this is the list I came up with. I hope you get some value out of it and maybe even consider some home improvements in your future. The second list is my "top ten things you can never have enough of for the kids." With your children in the home, there are certain items that you will go through very quickly and others that you want to have within arm's reach. This list is meant to save you from hunting around the house, making late-night runs to the store, and, in general, have happy children and an even happier mom and dad.

MY TOP TEN HELPFUL THINGS FOR YOUR HOME

If money were no object, here are the ten things I would recommend to you when it comes to choosing a home or key upgrades to your home. They will save you stress, time, or energy—and make your life a lot easier.

1. **Extra garage**—If you need one, get two. If you need two, get three. You will always need the space and envy those who have it.

2. **Closet space**—As I said, I would trade an extra bedroom for closets any day. The key to getting organized is having a place for everything, and you need closets to achieve that.

3. **Pantry**—If you want to stock up to save time, you need some place to put it. I love my big pantry, and would recommend it to anyone.

4. **Laundry room upstairs**—This is a new design theme in many new homes. We moved ours upstairs in the last year and I love it—no more going up and down stairs with a heavy basket full of clothes. It saves time and energy.

5. **Hot water dispenser**—This was in our house when we moved in, and it is awesome. You can warm up a bottle or defrost breast milk in no time. Have a cup of hot tea in seconds, and boiling water for pasta no longer takes half an hour.

6. **Mudroom**—Putting lockers into our mudroom was a godsend. All the coats, shoes, hats, gloves, and more are in one place, and I know where to find them. It also serves as the mail center. We get more junk mail than I know what to do with, but at least I have a space to put it before I have time to sort through all of it.

7. **Wireless Internet connection**—When you do need to log on from home, this saves so much time and allows you to be close to your children at the same time.

8. Great room—I love having the ability to make dinner and see my children at the same time. Even if it isn't the same room, having a family room attached to the kitchen is a great start.

9. Hard floors versus carpet—Children will get sick and spill many things in life. Rather than worry about the carpet staining I would recommend putting as many hard floors in your home as possible; hardwood, laminate, or tile are all good surfaces that are easy to clean and maintain.

10. Leather or microfiber furniture—These are easy-to-clean fabrics for the high-traffic areas in your home like the kitchen and family room.

TEN THINGS YOU CAN NEVER HAVE
ENOUGH OF FOR THE KIDS

1. **Spit-up clothes**—No matter how many you have, they never seem to be where you need them. At least having more helps improve your odds.

2. **Pacifiers**—Like the disappearing socks, these things can hide better than anything else I know of.

3. **Diaper bags**—I like to keep one in each car, one stocked in the house to give to grandparents or sitters, and one smaller-sized one to stick in the carriage for walks.

4. **Blankets**—The perfect gift for a second or third baby. Every child needs them and often becomes attached to them. We need to send them into daycare each week for naps, so it's always good to have a bunch.

5. **Diaper-changing stations**—Have multiple locations in your home. Why have to walk upstairs or down to change the diaper?

6. **Books**—The best thing you can do for your children is read to them often. We keep books everywhere in the house: family room, playroom, bedrooms, basement, car, etc.

7. **Five-minute meals**—Anything that can be made in less than five minutes: Budget Gourmet pastas, hot dogs, cheese sticks, sandwich meat, tuna fish, PB&J, soup. Great things to leave with sitters for them to make for kids.

8. **Pretreater**—Keep a stick in your diaper bag or purse, one on the hamper, and, of course, the laundry room. The commercials don't lie; kids seem to find every type of stain possible.

9. **Balls**—As Barney says, "It's the greatest toy of all." Children learn so much coordination from kicking, throwing,

hitting, or catching a ball. You can never have enough. Get soft ones for inside to limit potential damage.

10. Hugs and kisses—The more the merrier in our household. It teaches kids how to demonstrate their feelings while making you feel like a million bucks when you receive one.

DIVIDE RESPONSIBILITY FOR ALL KEY TASKS

To manage a dual-career household it is important to divide the household tasks between the husband and wife. Or, if you can afford it, outsource it. If you live with an extended family, then divide the tasks amongst the adults in the household. First, you and your husband should identify what tasks each of you don't mind doing and those tasks that you hate to do (see appendix E for a list to help you). For example, my husband does not like to grocery shop. Though he will go with me and the kids, he doesn't like to do it on his own. Likewise, I don't like to mow the lawn, so he does that. Arnie doesn't like to paint, so I handle all the painting duties. And so on, and so on.

Next, identify the tasks you severely dislike and would choose to outsource to someone else if you could afford to. Of course, outsourcing must be something that doesn't put hardship on your household, as the energy and time it saves can often be offset by the financial stress it causes. I found it useful to make our wish list for what we would outsource, starting with the most important and affordable and ending with the ideal state assuming money was not an issue. I have found in talking to more senior managers at P&G who are also dual-career couples, outsourcing becomes a much bigger part of managing the household over time, so it is great to identify which tasks would be outsourced. Some thought starters are:

- Housecleaning
- Lawn care
- Food preparation
- Painting
- Grocery shopping
- Party planning
- Home decorating

We decided to outsource housecleaning. Every other week we

have someone clean our house. The total annual cost is $3,000, including a holiday bonus. In addition to outsourcing the cleaning, I reduced my standard of clean after we had kids, as it wasn't a key priority for me. We chose to outsource cleaning over other household tasks because: 1) it saves us a lot of time each week, 2) it is very difficult to do deep cleaning (e.g., bathroom) with young children around, and 3) we both hate to clean! If you can't afford to outsource cleaning, consider quick-clean products (like Swiffer), which make some tasks much easier and faster.

Additionally, when we compared it to some of the other tasks above, they did not seem to give us the same benefits. Arnie does not mind mowing the lawn. It provides him some exercise and only takes two to three hours per week in the warm months, but would cost us as much or more than the housecleaning if we outsourced. The other tasks are not as regular in timing, so we can plan accordingly to ensure they get done in a timely manner and they often cost a lot more.

After you go through the common household duties and choose which tasks each of you will own, and identify the tasks you hate and can afford to outsource, any tasks that are left divide 50/50 with regards to who does them. For example, cooking would be left on our list, which means on some nights I cook, and on other nights Arnie cooks, usually based on who gets home first. ☺

ORGANIZATION IS CRITICAL

Being organized is essential in any dual-career household with children. Clutter, missed appointments, and disarray cause chaos and stress, and, frankly, waste a lot of time that you don't have. Having a place for everything brings comfort and makes the days and life run a lot more smoothly. It limits the time of having to find items and stress when you can't. I would tell any friend looking at new homes to trade an extra bedroom for more closet space any day of the week. A couple of areas in the home are more crucial than others when it comes to organization:

■ Mudroom—This is the first area of the home you enter when you arrive home. If this is cluttered the mess often spills over into other areas of the house. The best money I spent on my house was moving my laundry room up to the second floor (where all the dirty laundry is), and turning my laundry room into the ultimate mudroom. Before this my laundry room had shoes and lots of other "stuff" piled up in it so we would all trip over things when we entered the house. Our coat rack was ready to topple over from all the jackets on it, and, to find yours, you often had to remove four or five others! My solution was to create our mudroom. It has a mail center so all the mail and school papers come into one place, lockers for the kids, and a calendar to keep us all in line. The mail center includes a peg board where I can hang up school calendars, invitations, stamps, and other items that I need to refer to or "see" as a reminder of things to come in the future. I painted one wall with blackboard paint so we can write reminders or notes to one another. See photo on page 57. The lockers hold coats, umbrellas, shoes, hats, mittens, Baby Björn, snow pants, and more. In the future, book bags, sports equipment, and more will be housed here, helping us all stay a little more organized.

■ Basement—Even in homes with finished basements there is often a "rough" basement area where items can

Calendar   Lockers   Storage baskets

be stored. This is often the only "out of sight" area in your home, so you want to utilize it smartly. I store all my seasonal items, baby items, old paint, wine, and more in this area. Use plastic storage boxes to categorize items, labeling each of them so you can easily locate them.

■ Clothes closets—Regardless of the size, have a system to keep your closet organized. Separate clothes by type—pants, short skirts, long skirts, long-sleeve shirts, short-sleeve shirts, formal dresses, etc. If your closet is small, store off-season clothes in a plastic box in the basement. The vacuum storage bags are also a great space-saver and help protect your fabrics. Shoes should either be in their original box or some sort of shoe storage system. Buy a multi-hook hanger to put your belts on. This helps you see them and determine which are longer than others. On page 55 is a photo of our closet. The entire organization system was bought at Lowe's and installed by Arnie and me. As you can see, the important thing is to have a place for everything. Don't worry so much about how neat your folding is.☺

■ Fireproof safe—Every house should have a safe to store critical documents like your social security cards, birth certificates, will and trust documents, insurance policies, stocks and bond certificates, and more.

■ Garage—The garage typically stores a wider variety of items than any other area in your home, so it can get very messy very quickly. Try to divide your garage into sections to house the different items: garden items, tools, toys, strollers/wagons/bikes, sports equipment, etc. Utilize the walls to hang as many tools and other items that you don't want the kids to get into. Add additional shelving units and consider hanging a shelf from the ceiling as it frees up a lot of floor space. See page 55.

■ File cabinet—With online and credit card payments, the amount of statements you need to keep for records has

Sports equipment stored in garage

been reduced greatly; however, there are still key documents you need to hold on to. Get a file cabinet large enough to store these documents. Have a "tax document" file where you can dump all receipts from donations throughout the year to aid in your tax filing. It is also a good idea to have a paper shredder (I need to follow my own advice on this one!). With all of the issues around identity theft, simply shredding any mail or documents that have personal information is an easy way to try to protect your personal information.

Basements are great for storage.

Arnie's shirts and sweaters   Jo's skirts and dresses   Belts

Hanging shelf in garage

KEEP A MONTHLY HOUSEHOLD CALENDAR

In a busy household it is very easy for the left hand (your husband) to not know what the right hand (you) is doing. It is critical to co-ordinate all schedules (yours, his, and the kids) in one place that can be seen by everyone. I also recommend coordinating electronic cal-endars between spouses (see this in detail in career tips) so meetings are not booked on key dates, times, etc. Some of my friends and family members have different colors for each family member, or for different types of entries (appointments away from home, social events, kids activities, etc.). Figure out what system works for you and go with it. The most important thing is everyone knows where it is, feels ownership for updating it with key information, and knows who is responsible for what. When you have an event outside the house that requires a babysitter, put the sitter's name and time they are coming with the entry. Most erasable calendars only cover one month, so it is important to have a system for writing down appoint-ments that are further than a month out. I painted one of the walls in our mudroom with chalkboard paint so I can write our further-out appointments on this. Each month when I update my calendar, I check the chalkboard first to see what events we have that month. Here are some examples of key items to note on the calendar:

- Kids' activities (e.g., swim lessons, sport games)

- School activities (e. g., plays, concerts, PTA meetings, parent-teacher conferences, PJ day, field trips, bring-your-favorite-book-to-school day, etc.)

- Travel (note when you or your spouse is out of town)

- Social engagements (with sitter's name and time of arrival)

- Birthdays, anniversaries, weddings, and other engage-ments to remember

- Appointments: doctors, repairman, auto maintenance, hair cuts

- Grandparents' visits (to block the weekend for social activities or book activity if they love to sit the kids and let you go out!)

- Vacations and school holidays

Peg board   Blackboard

LIST, LIST, LIST, LIST, LIST

Nothing keeps you more organized than a good list. Unfortunately, unless you write it down there won't be any. Most people know lists as "to do" lists, which is a good start but there are all types of lists, many of which can be more fun to make. The first list you should have is a weekly to-do list, things that absolutely must get done for the household that week: appointments that need to be booked, bills that need to be paid, items that need to be purchased, events you need to attend, etc. This list should be updated for each week and should be coordinated with your monthly calendar so you can see out into the future what will need to be done. I also like to keep a list of future events, so once I register for a class for the kids, or commit to an evening out or meeting, I write it down so I can add it to the calendar and to-do list at the appropriate time.

The next "set" of lists should be shopping lists. Most of you should be familiar with the grocery shopping list. For years I didn't understand why people needed a list to go shopping, until I had a household to run and children to buy for. When it was just me, I bought what caught my fancy at the store. Now when I run out of a favorite item, I need to immediately write it down so I don't forget it, and the kids have a meltdown. I also find it easier to keep my shopping list by store. Being in the consumer-goods industry, I know which stores charge what, who takes a higher margin, etc. Because of this knowledge I buy certain products at certain stores. Groceries in one store, health and beauty aids in another, bulk items in another. Keeping a list by store helps me to stay organized, particularly since I don't go to the warehouse club on a regular basis. For key staples that your family can't do without, always buy more than one.

My friend Rini gave me a great tip about shopping lists. She has a list on her computer that she prints out each week, organized by aisle. As soon as she runs out of something she circles it on the list (which is on her refrigerator). She has blank lines to add non-regularly purchased items as needed. Another friend, Karen, plans her shopping lists around the meals she wants to make that week. She sits down to plan out the dinners and then makes her list based on what she needs for the meals. Figure out what system works best for you. The key is to have something to guide you in the store. Otherwise, it will take much longer, and I guarantee you will forget at least one item you had wanted to buy. I would recommend you make the list by store: for example, the grocery store, warehouse club, etc.

While the to-do list and shopping lists will save you time and stress, getting something done on the list doesn't really make you that happy. I like to keep additional lists of really fun subjects to keep me going and have something to look forward to. Here are some lists I suggest:

- **Gift wish list**—I gave my husband a list (typed in his BlackBerry) of potential gifts he could give me for my birthday, anniversary, Christmas, and so on. He always complained he didn't know what to give me, so I made the list for him. I suggest putting a wide range of items from low cost (like costume jewelry) to the ultimate wish (like diamond earrings), that way you have every type of occasion covered.

- **Vacation list**—We started keeping a list of places we wanted to go on vacation while we were in Europe. Not only did it allow us to dream of all the wonderful places we would love to visit, it was extremely helpful with planning the trips. This was especially true when we were told we were moving back to the U.S. We simply referred to our list and prioritized what we wanted to see before we returned to the U.S. Today I keep two vacation lists: 1) vacations we can take now with the kids, and 2) places we would like to go in the future when the kids are older.

- **Household project lists**—There is always some improvement or update you would like to make to your house—a new kitchen, new bathroom, paint a room, put pool in, get new appliances, clean the windows, hang a picture, etc. I keep a list of projects I need to do in the house, from big to small. When you have a day off, or a few extra minutes, or save the money needed, you can accomplish something on the list.

■ **Weekend activity list**—We love to go to different places with the kids on weekends and make it an adventure. Fall festivals in the autumn, amusement parks in the summer, and high school sporting events in the winter. Whatever the adventure, keep a list of fun community activities that the kids like and when they occur, so you never waste a minute saying, "What should we do today?" You can also simply create a folder to hold any articles or newspaper clippings on the events to keep all the information in one place.

■ **Thank yous**—If you have young kids in the house there are always thank-you notes to write. Since the year we were married I have had a set of thank yous to write each year; first the wedding, then Ben, then Claire, and now Sarah. Keep a list of thank yous you have to write to ensure you don't forget anyone. The worst feeling you can ever have is not remembering whether or not you sent a thank you (unless you find out you never did a few years later!).

■ **What to make for dinner**—Keep a short list of easy-to-make meals handy so you can consult it at 3:00 P.M. when the average woman begins to think...what should I make for dinner? (See appendix F.)

■ **School lists**—Names, e-mails, and numbers of all of your children's schools, teachers, and coaches. You may also want to keep a list of supplies needed.

■ **Sports lists**—Names, e-mails, and numbers of all coaches and teammates (if needed) for each sport league/team.

■ **Key dates list**—While I keep this online at Hallmark. com, you may want a list of all key family and friends events like birthdays, anniversaries, special events, holidays, and more.

■ **Clothes list**—Keep a short list of all the sizes of your children and husband: pants, shirts, skirts, shoes, belts, dress shirts, hat, etc. You can also keep a list of what they need so when someone asks you what they need for their birthday, you can tell them, along with the size (which is the next question).

Lists help you stay organized and motivated in many ways and require very little effort to create or maintain. I am a fan of the handwritten list rather than a list created on a computer or PDA as I like the feeling of crossing something off a list. The one negative with the old-fashioned paper list is they are easy to misplace. I can't tell you how much time I have spent looking for my list, only to have to recreate it on the way to the store! Consider using a notebook where the list can be stored or ripped out when needed. For lists that aren't used regularly, like a vacation list, consider using a Palm Pilot or BlackBerry if you have one so they are also on a computer as backup. Whatever method you choose, the key is to keep them updated, easy to access, and fun.

TAKE THE DAY AFTER A VACATION OFF

This is a recently discovered tip for me. Before we had kids, and even with just Ben, we would try to get every last minute of travel into our vacation. We would depart after work on Friday and take the last flight back home on Sunday, only to return to work first thing Monday morning. While we had the greatest amount of "vacation time" possible, on Monday it didn't really feel as if we had. We were exhausted, the house was a wreck (as we only had time to dump our bags before heading to bed), the laundry was knee deep, and often Ben was a bit off-kilter because his schedule was thrown for a loop.

When booking a trip to the West Coast last year, I decided I would take Monday off as well, just in case the kids had some jet lag. They didn't, but the difference of having Monday off was amazing. I was able to unpack, do the laundry, go grocery shopping (given that the frig was empty after ten days away), go through the mail, return phone calls to those who left messages, and allow the kids to sleep in if necessary. It also gave me time to go through my work e-mail so I wouldn't be hit by the 250-300 messages that I would normally come back to after a week off. Yes, it is an extra day of vacation spent, but well worth it. You'll go back to work well rested, not stressed about e-mail, knowing your home is in order, and your children have adjusted to being home and back in their routine.

NEVER WALK UPSTAIRS EMPTY HANDED

This tip is as old as I am, in that it comes from my mom. My parents' home, which is the same home I grew up in (and my mom has lived in since she was sixteen), is not very large. Yet despite its size, it was the busiest home in the neighborhood. Everyone hung out at our house. My mom wanted the home to be comfortable to everyone who entered it, so she would constantly organize things and remove any clutter that existed, usually putting the items that had been dumped on the floor or tables at the foot of the steps. This was our sign to take them upstairs, following her rule of "never walk upstairs empty handed."

When Arnie and I moved into our home I implemented this rule. To make it a bit easier for us, and increase its impact on our time, our rule became "never walk up or downstairs empty handed." To remind us to do this I have baskets at the top and bottom of the stairs to help move the items since often they are small toys, gadgets, or shoes that our darling little ones leave behind. The key to making this work and saving yourself time and chaos from the mess it creates, is to get in the habit of looking for items that belong on the other floor of the home. Here are some things I look for:

- Shoes—often left by the door or sofa
- Toys—we have "upstairs" toys and "downstairs" toys that often end up in the wrong place
- Clothes—dirty or clean laundry, jackets deposited on the floor
- Paperwork—bills or key documents that need to be filed (which for us is upstairs)
- Groceries—purchased items to be brought upstairs after purchase
- Books/magazines/newspapers—to be recycled when they are read, or given away

STOCK UP ON STAPLE GOODS FOR THE HOUSEHOLD

I must admit, this one comes really easy to me. I'm not sure why, but the thought of running out of a staple good frightens me to death. It must be my type A personality. On top of this, I am a warehouse-club junkie and love a good bargain. When you combine all of these traits, you have closets and pantries full of a backup supply of product. When you are managing a full-time job and caring for children, running to the store because you are out of toilet paper is stress you don't need. It is also a waste of precious time that you could be playing with the kids, spending time with your husband, or taking time for you. By keeping a stock of key products in the home, you reduce the number of these trips and save a ton of time. Here is a list of items and brands I recommend keeping backup stock of:

- Bathroom items: toothpaste, toothbrushes, shampoo, conditioner, bodywash/soap, shaving cream, razors, vitamins, Tampax, Always, makeup, deodorant, Q-tips, saline solution, Charmin, air fresheners, lotion

- Medicines: children's Tylenol, cold medicine, Pepto-Bismol, aspirin, Tylenol, Advil, allergy medicine, Mylacon, children's Orajel.

- Baby Needs: Pampers, wipes, formula, Desitin ointment, baby lotion, baby wash

- Cleaning items: Dawn, Cascade, Tide, Downy, Bounce, Swiffer, Mr. Clean, Soft Scrub, furniture polish, Bounty, sponges, bleach, window cleaner, carpet cleaner

- Food items: soup, pasta, pasta sauce, snacks for kids, oatmeal, cereal, frozen waffles, frozen ravioli, cake mix, mustard, ketchup, mayo, peanut butter, jelly, salad dressing, ʾide dishes (like rice, pasta sides, etc.), chicken breast, ʾound beef, spices, chicken nuggets, mac 'n' cheese

If you stock up on these items, you should only have to shop for them a few times per year (except those with expiration dates), which allows you to get them on sale or in bulk which reduces the cost. Of course, you do need to have the storage space to hold the items, which can be a problem. Don't be afraid to use the garage or basement if needed.

LEARN TO OPERATE WITH ONLY ONE HAND

Of course the best case is to have both your hands to work with as you're cooking, cleaning, driving, putting your makeup on. Most daily tasks are much easier and safer when done with two hands. However, with a child or multiple children in the home this is often a luxury you don't have. You can try a Baby Björn or other sling-like carrier that allows you to have both hands free while keeping the baby happy by being close to your body, but in many instances you are doing a quick task and don't have the time to put the carrier on. Experiment with different positions and find the one most comfortable to you and be very careful, particularly when you are cooking and around hot objects. Once you are comfortable you will be able to prepare meals, empty the dishwasher, unload groceries, brush your teeth, put makeup on, get the mail, put the laundry into the dryer, refill juice cups, and much more all with one hand, allowing you to be very productive while keeping your little one happy.

UTILIZE YOUR MATERNITY LEAVE

While the main goal of your maternity leave should be to nurture your newborn and bond with him or her, you can also utilize it to accomplish other goals. After the first couple of months, you and your new addition will settle into a nice routine. A big part of this routine will be naps for the little one, which leaves plenty of time for you. Even if the child is not napping, he can be swinging in the swing, playing in a baby play saucer, playing on the Gymini mat, or cooing at the mobile while you do tasks around the house. Being home rather than in the office allows you to accomplish a lot of tasks or projects around the house that can't get done without you present in person.

Keep a list of house projects that need to get done. From large projects that require contractors to small projects like hanging a picture, always keep a list handy. In the case that it requires a contractor of some kind, be sure to contact them well in advance of your due date to get cost estimates and availability. This will ensure the work can get done while you are home and that you have the necessary funds in case you need to apply for a loan. Here are some examples of the household projects we have done during our four (three for Joanna and one for Arnie) leaves:

- Had trees removed
- Installed sprinkler system
- Moved laundry room from main floor to upstairs
- Had lockers built and installed for mudroom
- Picked fabrics for draperies
- Enlarged patio
- Installed shelving in garages
- Painted or wallpapered
- Mulched and cleaned up landscaping around home
- Decorated for holidays

- Installed sound system in the house
- Scheduled car maintenance appointments
- Upgraded cable and digital phone hookup

You can also utilize your leave to get better organized around the home and take care of other household tasks or jobs that you never find the time to do. For those of you who do not like to do this type of work in the home, I have a friend (thanks, Kristi) who has used and would recommend a "home manager" to help. For $15-20 per hour (Cincinnati pricing), this person will help do household tasks like cooking, gardening, cleaning, laundry, and more. Here are some thought starters regarding home management on leave:

- Organize the pantry, shelves, drawers in kitchen

- Organize your closets, put seasonal clothes away or get them out of storage (add things to your list of what is needed as you do this)

- Clean your oven or refrigerator (a friend gave me a tip: clean two shelves each week, keep rotating the two shelves you do, then it never becomes a big job)

- Clean your windows
- Clean and organize your garage

Finally, you should definitely utilize your leave for yourself and your family. Think about those things you always wished you had the time to do and take advantage of your leave. You will be exhausted at times, so what better way to pick yourself up than to have some fun during this wonderful time. For me, I chose to write a book, but I have friends and family that have done the following:

- Plan or take a vacation
- Take language lessons
- Garden
- Exercise

- Join a play group
- Take cooking lessons and try some new recipes

All of the above requires time that is often hard to find if you take a very short leave. If you can afford it, I recommend taking an extended leave. I have had three maternity leaves of ten months, four months, and eight months. The four-month leave was by far the most stressful and least productive. As I mentioned earlier in the book, I had just returned to work after taking ten months with Ben when I got pregnant. Given that I had just returned, I didn't feel comfortable taking a long maternity leave. While my company encouraged me to do what was right, I just didn't feel I could take another long leave. We decided I would take a short leave, and they would hold my job for me and not replace me. My husband was due to move to a new role soon after the baby was born, so we decided he would take a three-month leave to help out. In hindsight I would not recommend a short leave to anyone, particularly if you are returning to your same role. I was constantly torn about how much I should stay involved at work. The people who worked for me were neglected, and hence required an incredible amount of attention when I returned. This situation made my return very stressful. Projects I thought would move forward hadn't, and others were in a different place than I expected. In the end I felt like I hit a brick wall when I returned and had tenfold the amount of stress.

On the other hand, my longer leaves were taken "in between assignments." I finished an assignment and then went on leave. This allowed me to completely walk away from work and concentrate on my baby and other projects. The more time I had, the more I got accomplished at home and on my personal projects (like this book). I realize this is often a decision based on finances more than anything, but I would truly encourage you to save up to allow you to spend precious time with your baby and take a much needed break from work so you can rest. ☺

KEEP A SUM OF CASH ON HAND

In today's society there are very few things that require cash as payment versus credit card, debit card, or check. But they still exist. For our household we need cash for our maid and babysitters. In the spirit of keeping it simple, instead of running to the ATM and taking out money each week or couple of weeks, I recommend keeping a sum of cash in the house. This limits last-minute runs to the ATM on the way home from a night out to pay the babysitter, as well as the frustration when you can't find your bank's ATM and have to pay a fee or, worse yet, simply can't find one. Once a month or as needed, stop at the bank on a Saturday and withdraw a bulk sum of cash that will meet your needs, and keep it stored in a safe place. For purchases that don't require cash, I would encourage you to use your credit card as much as possible. This allows you to keep better track of your spending and helps with budget keeping in Quicken or other software tools. Often you can also get an additional benefit like cash back, airline miles, etc.

EASY-TO-COOK DINNERS

The only thing worse than cooking dinner is thinking about what to make for dinner. I often find myself driving home from work wondering, "What am I going to make for dinner?" As a dual-career family you have to make decisions as to what is really important to you and where you are going to spend your limited time. For me, when it comes to meals for my family, the most important thing is we eat a hot meal together each night. It doesn't matter to me if it is a homemade recipe made from scratch or a frozen pizza, so long as we can enjoy it together and the children are getting the nutrition they need. We do try to limit the amount we eat out as it can be very stressful with young children, not to mention expensive. To make things easier on me I use two tools:

1. A handy list of easy-to-make meals (in my BlackBerry)

2. A stock of easy-to-make meals in the house.

For the easy-to-make meals, think about meals your mom made or meals you really like and jot them down. Often it isn't the meal itself that takes time and effort so much as thinking about it and finding all the ingredients. When I was on my first maternity leave I began to cook a lot. I was in Europe where you shopped daily or every other day for fresh produce and meat, as they do not have as many preservatives in the food. This forced me to plan meals and think about what to make. They also don't have "pre-prepared" convenient-to-make meals like we do in America. I found that these meals weren't that difficult and many could be made in advance, so I started to keep a list. Here is my list:

- Meatloaf
- Pasta (with meatballs, sausage, primavera, lasagna, etc.)
- Chicken marsala, chicken parmesan, lemon chicken
- Frittata or quiche
- Breakfast for dinner (French toast, pancakes, omelettes, etc.)

- Burritos/tacos/quesadillas
- Potato soup
- Beef stew
- Stuffed eppers
- Grilled meat with corn on cob and salad

Here in the U.S. we have a large array of easy-to-prepare or pre-prepared meals. My hat is off to the people at General Mills, Kraft Foods, Nestlé, ConAgra, and others. They have truly made food preparation very quick and easy and offer a huge variety. I have no qualms, nor should you, about putting a "pre-prepared" meal on the table for my family. They taste good, are less expensive than eating out, and can be made in less than thirty minutes. Here are some of our favorites that I recommend:

- Stouffer's Skillet Sensations
- Stouffer's frozen meals (lasagna, stuffed pepper, meatloaf)
- Frozen tortellini, frozen ravioli, frozen stuffed shells (any brand)
- Betty Crocker Slow Cooker Helpers
- Michael Angelo's Chicken Piccata
- Lipton-Knorr pasta and rice sides
- Betty Crocker potatoes: au gratin, scallop, etc.
- Pot stickers
- Frozen pizza
- Campbell's Supper Bakes and Dessert Bakes

After a really stressful workday, my husband and I will often revert to our college days and make breakfast for dinner (the kids love it). This meal can be as simple as cereal or scrambled eggs. It is a nice change and extremely easy to make on those days when you can barely walk and talk at the same time.

SUNDAY NIGHT COOKING

I have found Sunday nights to be quite unique and important. Unlike weeknights where you have a limited amount of time between getting home and putting the kids to bed, Sunday you often start cooking much earlier. It is different from Saturday night as Saturday is typically the night you will go out with your husband and get a sitter, so you aren't home to get things done. This all makes Sunday very valuable to you, and you want to take advantage of the extra time.

For me I have made Sunday night my cooking night. I try to cook at least two meals each Sunday night, one for that evening and one for later in the week. I also cook a larger than normal meal for Sunday evening so I know we will have leftover food for another evening during the week where time is more limited. Here are a few tips to make this easy on you. First, think ahead about what you want to make and shop for the appropriate ingredients on your normal weekend grocery-shopping trip. This will make it much easier on Sunday knowing you have all the necessary ingredients on hand. Second, try to make a meal that can be reheated easily as you won't have an hour during the week to reheat the meal. Third, start cooking earlier in the day, around four or five o'clock, so you can sit down for dinner a bit earlier. This allows you more time in the evening to get some other household tasks done like sorting the mail, paying bills, and so on.

CAKE MIX, JELL-O, AND READY-TO-BAKE COOKIES

While I liked to bake around the holidays before I had kids, I now love to make yummy desserts all the time so my family can enjoy them, especially when I am pregnant. Desserts are also the perfect bribe to have in the house. ☺ Today's cake and cookie mixes are either completely pre-made (like ready-to-bake cookies) or require simple ingredients like milk, eggs, or water. In less than an hour, you have a warm dessert—it really can't get much simpler. In fact, it is so simple I like to let the kids help me. It teaches them coordination (pouring milk), measurements, basic cooking, and keeps them happily close to you. Always try to have mixes and icing on hand so you are prepared for birthdays, play dates, neighborhood gatherings, or a precious request from your little one. Jell-O is also an easy way to have a low-fat dessert around for all to enjoy! Watch it jiggle and the kids giggle.

MULTIPLE HAMPERS SO YOU DON'T HAVE TO SORT CLOTHES

Laundry is a necessary evil in every household (unless it is a task you decide to hire out), and one that is very near and dear to me, given that I was the Bounce brand manager. ☺ It is also a time-consuming multi-step process, including: 1) sorting, 2) pretreating, 3) washing, 4) drying, 5) folding, 6) ironing if necessary, 7) storage/putting away. The most-hated task (per P&G research) is ironing, followed by folding. Try to buy as many non-iron fabrics as possible to reduce the amount of ironing you have to do. We have been really happy with Brooks Brothers shirts (sold at the outlet) and Van Heusen trousers for men (which we got at Costco for $24.99). Unfortunately, I don't have any time savers for folding. The area I do save a lot of time in is sorting (it also helps reduce the risk of color bleeding).

I have three hampers in my closet that help do the sorting for me. We have a colored-clothes hamper, white-clothes hamper, and dry-cleaning hamper. Some households like to sort light and dark clothes, so you could use the third hamper for this if you don't do a lot of dry cleaning. For the kids' clothes, I have a separate hamper to allow me to wash their clothes separately when they are younger before I use regular detergent on them. By having multiple hampers all I need to do is dump the hamper into the washer, no sorting needed, saving me at least fifteen to thirty minutes from my laundry routine. Most organization stores like Hold Everything and Organized Living sell units on wheels with multiple hampers in them, providing another solution to the sorting problem.

PRETREATERS IN KEY AREAS

While I love Tide (remember who I work for ☺) and know it cleans very well, nothing will get out food stains, paint stains, and other messes children get on their clothes if it sits too long. I have learned this the hard way, ruining many clothes because I forgot to pre-treat the stain in a timely fashion because once it settles in, there is no getting it out! In an effort to catch the stains, I keep pretreaters in key areas:

- Diaper bag—I keep a Tide stain pen, a Clorox Bleach Pen, and Spray 'n Wash stick in my main diaper bag along with spare clothes so I can take the clothes off and treat the stain.

- Hamper—I have a Spray 'n Wash spray bottle in the nursery next to the hampers so I can treat clothes before I put them into the hamper.

- Laundry room—I keep another spray bottle in the laundry to retreat before I put them in the wash.

This isn't a lot of extra work and will save you lots of time re-washing items. It will also keep your clothes looking newer longer so you can pass them down to the next little addition.

LEATHER FURNITURE AND STAINGUARD

There aren't many guarantees in life, but one thing that I can guarantee any parent is that your child will either spill food, spit up, or wipe their drool/snot on your furniture. Given the expense of furniture, most families would like to keep their furniture beyond the baby/infant/preschool years. With this in mind I have found leather and microfiber fabrics to be lifesavers. Leather is easy to wipe off and resists wear and tear. Microfiber is very comfortable and can be treated with Stainguard, allowing you to wipe off any stain or unzip it and run it through the wash. Most fabrics can have Stainguard added to them. In our home we have velvet, microfiber, and cotton sofas all treated with Stainguard. For a couple of hundred dollars it will save you many headaches and extend the longevity of your furniture. I have included some photos below and on the next page to help illustrate all the different styles you can have and still let kids live a little fun.

Leather bar stools

Microfiber couch treated with Stainguard

RUN ERRANDS AS A FAMILY

Don't be afraid to run your errands as a family. While you may think the last thing you want to do is take your kids grocery shopping, when you have a spouse along to help, it can actually be a nice experience that you all enjoy (well, maybe not your husband). I found myself away from my kids for hours on end each weekend while I ran my errands, only to come home to an exhausted and sometimes frustrated husband as he had to deal with the kids on his own. To try to reduce some of the stress I began taking Ben along, and he really liked it—all the sights and colors, helping me get things off the shelf, and, of course, getting to sit in the cart. We turned it into a family affair once Sarah was born as she had to come with me to be nursed, and I liked having the helping hands to make things a bit easier. Additionally, as they got older, Ben and Claire would fight us about going down for a nap. We began to plan our errands so that they would fall asleep in the car. Arnie would take a magazine to read and stay with them as I shopped. This way they got some rest, and everyone had a little peaceful time.

Sometimes we leave early to go out to lunch and enjoy a nice day. Be careful not to get into the habit of buying something each trip for your children. This is a very slippery slope. If you do need to purchase an item for your children, let them know ahead of time that you are making a special trip to look for their new sneakers or coat. This gets them very excited and makes the trip easier as they aren't distracted by other items (as you can say, "Remember we are here to get new sneakers, not ...").

In the end I have found that my errand running may take a little longer if the kids stay awake, but we get to spend family time together, the kids get to experience different environments and persons as well as learn about where we buy certain items and how things work (like how mail is sent at the post office).

DIRTY-CLOTHES SUITCASE

While on vacation be sure to keep all your dirty clothes together. We have found it easiest to place them in one of the empty suitcases (or two or three). As an alternative you can also take a kitchen garbage bag for the dirty clothes. This approach makes it much easier when you are packing to come home as all the dirty clothes are together and, more importantly, separate from the clean clothes that haven't been worn, so they stay clean in transit. It also makes the unpacking much easier as you simply take that suitcase straight to the laundry room and wash the clothes. No pulling out dirty clothes from every family member's suitcase to then carry them to the laundry room. You'll save a lot of time and stress on the end of a wonderful vacation, keeping the relaxation going a little longer once you get home.

PREPARE FOR THE BABY TO ARRIVE

This tip is much more useful for the second or third child, as I think most parents are *overly* prepared for their first due to all the excitement and the incredible marketing done by the baby industry. However, with your hands full with your other children you may find it easy to be somewhat unprepared for your expanding family. Here are some tips to make sure you're prepared. About two months before your due date make sure you have done the following:

- Transition your older child to her new room, new car seat, out of high chair, etc. Transitions are always difficult and can often take some time so you want to make sure you allow for it.

- Baby clothes—Make sure you take out your infant clothes (0-3 and 3-6 months) and wash them to have them ready for baby so you save time later. Don't forget blankets too.

- Car seat—Take the infant seat out of storage, wash it, install in car, etc.

- Bedding—Wash all bedding for cradle, crib, portable crib, bassinet, Moses basket, etc.

Around one month prior to your due date:

- Diapers—Stock up on newborn and size-1 diapers.
- Bottles—If you will bottle feed, get bottles out and put number-0 nipples back on them. Be sure to stock up on formula as well.
- Insurance—Print out paperwork to add your new addition to insurance.
- Cameras—Make sure all batteries are charged and cameras ready.
- Finalize plan for who will take care of your children when you go into labor.

Tips and Time Savers:

For Managing the Children

When children enter your life, you suddenly go from a couple to a family. More importantly you move from being an almost completely independent person to having another human being completely dependent on you. This is a daunting task. Every day this precious life is reliant on you to feed him, bathe him, dress him, entertain him, and so on. The result of this is what will seem like a completely new daily life for you and your husband. I hope these tips will help you become more prepared for the baby to arrive, have a happier and more restful maternity leave, get out of the house a little faster and happier each morning, stay a little more organized, and make your weekends more rewarding than exhausting.

FLEXIBILITY IS KEY

It may seem a bit odd that this tip is preceding the next one of "routine, routine, routine," but it was a deliberate choice. While you need to establish a routine for the sake of the children and yourself, it is even more essential that you are flexible within that routine. So while you may feed the baby or children at the same time each day to ensure they are nourished and don't have a meltdown, be flexible in where you feed them. You could run errands as a family and go out to eat, allowing you to accomplish something while sticking to a routine. Your baby can just as easily nap while you are walking in the park and getting some exercise as they can in their crib at home. You will be much better off, as will your children, if you are flexible and "go with the flow" regarding the routine versus being ultra-regimented. If you are too strict with your routine, you run the risk of your children not being comfortable outside of their normal setting. For example, they may be unable to nap outside of the home, or in an environment that is not perfectly quiet. Given the small amount of time you have to accomplish your tasks, this would become extremely limiting and also create an unhappy child at some point. *Be flexible and honor the routine versus a schedule, and everyone will be better off in the end.*

ROUTINE, ROUTINE, ROUTINE

The key to keeping you and your children sane when they are young is establishing a routine. Children need some regularity in their lives, so the sooner you can establish a routine for them the better. Once you have a routine it is critical that you don't disrupt it too often, as your children rely on it, and major disruptions can throw them off and create behavioral problems. For our first child we turned to a book that was recommended to us by various people we respected and trusted. That book was *On Becoming Babywise* by Gary Ezzo and Robert Bucknam. Not having experience with a newborn, and living abroad away from family and friends, we found comfort in having a book to refer to when it came to the baby's eating and sleeping habits.

The key thing behind routines is to recognize them. Watch your child to learn what their actions and behaviors are telling you. Over time you will recognize when they are hungry, tired, wet, or in pain. Once you recognize each behavior, take note of when it is occurring. Before long you will see a routine forming before your eyes—when they want to eat or sleep, when they have a bowel movement, when they wake up, when they are happiest, and when they are crankiest. Now, a routine *does not* and *should not* shackle you to your home. In order to make a dual-career lifestyle work and to manage a household, you need flexibility (which I will get to). So remember routine means a schedule that you can execute in many different ways and places.

Once your child is in a routine it is really important you don't change it or disrupt it, especially when another child is born. Most often in dual-career homes the older children are in daycare or with a nanny. Whatever the childcare situation, it is crucial you do not change it when a new baby is born as your older children rely on this routine for their sense of normalcy. Bringing a new baby into the home is a big change for children to deal with, so you do not want to change their routine on top of this. Let them handle one transition at a time. This doesn't mean you can't keep the children home for a day or two when the baby is born, especially if grandparents are in town. However, you don't want to keep them out for too long as getting them back to school could be difficult once they realize Mom is home all day. Remember to budget for childcare accordingly. If you are on maternity leave, often you are not earning an income for a portion of the time. Be sure to budget for daycare even when you are not working to allow for the routine to be maintained.

COUNT TO TEN OR WALK AWAY

No matter how strong your parenting or negotiating skills, all children have meltdowns every now and then. The key thing is to recognize when you can help in some way versus those times when you just need to walk away. Often children simply need something from you and are having a difficult time communicating it. Given that every child's speech develops differently, I wouldn't recommend a wait-and-see approach with regards to your child's communication skills, hoping they can speak early (which is around eighteen months). You could try to teach your child sign language to help limit the meltdowns. We have done this with our children at a very basic level, teaching them signs related to key areas like: hungry, thirsty, more, all done, tired, hot, please, thank you, cat, dog, fish, and other animals (to have some fun too). This at least lets your children tell you some of their needs at a much younger age. In hindsight, I wish I had taught our second child more signs. Our first, Ben, could speak very clearly and had a broad vocabulary at eighteen months. Claire, on the other hand, didn't really start talking until two, but she signed much better. Had we taught her more signs than we did Ben, we would have saved a lot of stress.

On the other hand, many tantrums have nothing to do with basic needs like eating, so basic signing won't help you. In these cases it is very easy to get frustrated because often you don't know what the child needs or have enough hands to fulfill their demands quickly. I found that I would often explode only making the issue worse. When my son started to pick up on the fact that I was yelling and he didn't like it (and told me so), I realized I needed to change and be careful how I reacted. I began to walk out of the room and count to ten, then return and try to solve the issue. Many times the situation solved itself in this time. Ironically, I got the idea from *The Doodlebops* show on *Playhouse Disney* where they sing a song "Count to Ten."

Here is a perfect example. One morning we were going through our normal breakfast routine. I made waffles for Ben and Claire and gave them each a bowl of grapes and juice. Typically while they are eating, I get Sarah's cereal and fruit ready and feed her. As I was trying to prepare Sarah's cereal, Claire started screaming that she wanted a Go-GURT too (even though three minutes earlier she didn't choose that option). The kitchen was more cluttered than normal as we were leaving for vacation the next day, and I had snacks and other items out to be packed. I told Claire to hold on a few minutes but that didn't work. Sarah was then cranky from hunger as she sat in her high chair. I decided to help Claire first and tried to grab a Go-GURT quickly only to knock some cookies off the shelf in the refrigerator, and they broke all over the floor. I knew I was about to lose it, so I walked into the pantry and counted to ten. Yes, Sarah got a bit more upset, Claire still yelled, and the cookies were still on the floor, but I was calm and in a better state to face the kids. Just one minute later, and all was well. Walk away and take a moment; everyone will be better off in the end.

JOIN ORGANIZATIONS
FOR CHILDREN'S ACTIVITIES

You always want to have fun activities to do as a family on the weekend or day off (see the tip on keeping lists). We have found it most efficient to become members of two or three organizations each year that our children really enjoy. When your children are infants, toddlers, or preschool-age, some of the best activities are the local zoo, children's museum, aquarium, or puppet/children's theater. We are also fortunate enough to have a local amusement park that caters to younger children. As they get older, look into the larger amusement parks as they often have "kiddy" areas as well as rides that cater to older children, so you can continue to enjoy it as they grow.

The great thing about membership is it is very cost-efficient. Our zoo membership (roughly $120 annually for the family, including parking) pays for itself in less than three visits. We go at least once per month so it is very cost-efficient. When you become members they also have reciprocal deals with other zoos or museums throughout the country where you get discounted or free admission. For example, when in New York this past December we went to the Mid-Hudson Children's Museum with the kids and got in free because we were members of the Cincinnati Museum Center (about $120 per year for four museums and parking). Finally, you never feel guilty about going or leaving when you are a member. Even if the kids have a meltdown twenty minutes into the trip, it's no big deal to pack things up and leave because you didn't open your wallet to go.

TRANSITION ROOMS
BEFORE THE BABY ARRIVES

Even though the baby likely will sleep in your room for the first weeks or months, it's important to transition your toddler or preschooler before the baby arrives. If you wait until the baby is here, the child may resent the baby for making her "leave" her room and will associate any emotions with the move with the baby. Take the time to make a big deal about the move and going to a big-boy or big-girl room. Let the child pick out something for the room— bedding, a rug, a lamp, something to hang on the wall, the paint color, or a toy. This will help him get comfortable with and feel good about the move.

Additionally, while you may have a plan for when you will transition rooms, your child may have a different plan in mind. For example, I had planned on moving Ben into his big-boy room in March (he would be eighteen months) with Claire due in April. Unfortunately, after spending the Christmas holiday in New York in a different sleeping place, he decided he didn't want to sleep in his crib anymore. He flat out rejected his crib. For one week I slept with him on the guest-room double bed, trying to transfer him into his crib after he was in a deep sleep, but he woke up each time. After a week of this routine we decided to put the double mattress on the floor in the room that would be his big-boy room to begin the transition. I quickly ordered furniture that ended up being delivered while I was in early labor with Claire (she came three weeks early). ☺

The moral of the story is: begin the transition sooner than you need to just to make sure you have enough time. Your goal should be to have your child happy and settled into the new space well in advance of the baby's arrival. This will also reduce the activity and stress on your body and mind after the baby is born.

FOLLOW YOUR GUT, NOT THE BOOKS

This is a really hard one to write given that I am writing a "tip book" myself. But that is the problem with most baby books—they don't feel like "tip books" but instead like the Holy Grail of child rearing. The key to reading any book about being pregnant or having an infant/child is to take them as guidance, not as a directive. If you try to follow every step and piece of advice or worry about every little thing that your baby isn't doing at the precise time she should be doing it, you will drive yourself crazy. In my opinion, most baby books can make you feel like you are doing something wrong or inadequately, causing more worry than help.

My advice is to follow your gut. Ask a lot of questions of people like you who have been in your shoes before and who you trust. Listen to their responses, and do what feels right. Getting to know your "baby gut" is like getting to know a manual transmission. I remember when I was trying to learn how to drive a stick shift in high school. My father saw me struggling and told me to "listen to the car." At first I thought he was crazy, but when I continued to stall on every hill, I tried his advice, listened to the engine sounds, and soon became a master. I believe the same advice could be given to every new mother: "listen to your baby." Babies have different cries for when they are hungry, tired, wet, or ill. It will take awhile but you will be able to recognize these cries before you know it. You will also be able to recognize a little cold and sniffle versus something more serious. You'll recognize a stomach virus and the symptoms and know exactly how long it will last for each child. Your natural gut as a mother is *very* strong. Nurture it and have confidence in it; you and your baby will be less neurotic and happier for it.

If you can't assess a situation, get advice from someone you trust. For me this is my mom or sister. Despite being miles away, they can still listen to me as I describe the symptoms and give me their advice about what to do. I could call the doctor, but often you have to tell a receptionist all the information only to tell a nurse all over again when they call back. Just like in the game "telephone," many things get lost in translation. I would rather call someone I know and trust and let them talk me through it.

KEEP STORAGE BOXES IN EACH CHILD'S CLOSET

This tip will serve as a time saver, organizational tool, and heart-string tugger. You will need two boxes per child, roughly two-by-two-by-three feet. The first bin is used to store clothes that your child has outgrown. As soon as you notice your child is too big for the item, place it in the box. Don't worry about folding it as you will better organize the bin when it is full and ready to go into storage. Remember to place shoes, hats, mittens, coats, and other items

CLAIRE'S CLOTHES BIN

in the box as well. When it is full, better organize the items as they may be in storage for a while. I recommend laying items flat, keeping shoes in boxes, and placing all socks, mittens, hats, and so on in a plastic bag to keep them together. When finished, label the box so you know what is in there without looking. I use the system of gender and clothes size, for example; Boy 0-3 months, Boy 12-18 months, Girl 2T/3T, etc. Store all the boxes in the same location so you can easily find what you are looking for when the second or third child arrives; you hand down the clothes to a niece, nephew or friend; or choose to sell the items.

The second bin is the "keepsake" bin. This will serve as an easy-access place to keep all those items you want to save for your child to have when he grows up. Each time you come across something you think you should save, just toss it in (again don't worry about it being neat and organized). This will also limit the clutter around your house. As a thought starter for you, here is a list of some of the items I have in my keepsake boxes:

- Baby books and first-year calendars
- Baby blankets and personalized towels
- Christening or other religious items
- Baby and family pictures (I keep every Christmas photo)
- Copy of birth announcement and other key documents from their lives
- Ticket stubs from various events
- Artwork, progress reports, journals from daycare, and report cards

This is an extremely easy way to give back to your children by documenting the key things from their childhood. It is also a great way to reminisce and bring back fond memories as your sort through and organize it over time.

CLAIRE'S KEEPSAKE BIN

KEEP SNACKS IN YOUR CAR

You and your children will spend a lot of time in your car, particularly if your childcare is outside of the home. You will also find that your children are often hungry in the car. Perhaps it is the end of a long day at school or the middle of a long afternoon of running errands. Whatever the time or reason, the easiest solution is to keep a stock of snacks in your car. I have a storage bin in both cars filled with a variety of snacks, some healthy and some not so healthy. I also recommend having a stock of baby wipes with you to take care of messy hands and faces. Here are some of our snack favorites:

- Fruit snacks
- Pretzels
- Nutri-grain bars
- Breakfast bars
- Cookies
- Cheese crackers

SNACK BIN

SOMETHING TO HOLD THE BABY ON EVERY FLOOR

Keeping the baby occupied for short periods of time allows you to keep yourself and the household running. Make sure you have something you can safely put the baby into on each floor to make this easier on you and the baby. This can be a baby seat, baby play saucer, car seat, high chair, or other helpful inventions. I find it most helpful to keep our vibrating baby seat upstairs in the master bath. When I need to get ready, take a shower, get Ben or Claire to brush their teeth or take a bath, I can put Sarah in the seat and keep her happy. On the main floor we have a baby play saucer and booster seat to keep her happy. I prefer to have her in the baby play saucer so she can play but the booster seat (Bumbo) is great because it allows her to sit and watch her brother or sister in any location. Finally we have another baby play saucer in the basement.

This may seem excessive but it saves time moving the items around and keeps the baby happy. I actually bought both of our baby play saucers used (from other American ex-pats) while we were in Europe for less than $20 each. You also don't have to get the fancy baby seats. While we have a vibrating one, all of our children prefer the nonvibrating one, and it cost significantly less. Once Upon a Child (national consignment franchise) is a great place to look for used items, as well as local yard sales.

My friend Kristi gave me another great tip. Keep some toys for the baby wrapped up in a small comforter or large blanket. When you need to move to another room (with the baby) you simply pick up the comforter and move it to the next room, bringing your mini-playroom along with you. This also minimizes your cleanup as you simply fold it up and stick it in the corner somewhere when you are finished.

INFANT CAR SEAT (FISHER PRICE)

BOUNCY SEAT (FISHER PRICE)

TAKE CLOTHES OUT FOR THE WEEK AHEAD

I do most of the children's laundry over the course of the weekend. I fold the clothes after each load and create three piles in a laundry basket. I *do not* put the clothes away until all the clothes have been washed and folded. Once I am done, I then move to the kids' rooms. Before putting away their pile of clothes, I pick out five outfits for the week ahead, and pair them with underwear and the appropriate socks/tights. Each pile is stacked on top of one another. After I have the clothes for the week ahead, I hang the clean clothes up or put them in their respective drawers. Then I move onto the next room until I am done. This entire routine takes me less than thirty minutes and saves me so much time and stress as I just have to grab the clothes each night (see next tip). This also makes life easy on my husband, in-laws, or parents who care for the children when I am traveling.

As your kids get older, this tip comes in handy when they decide: "I don't want to wear that today." If any of my children are not happy with the outfit I have picked out for that day, I tell them they can go into their room and choose another outfit from the pile. This gives them some choice but doesn't add a lot of time to our morning routine. It also helps them understand limits, as they know they will need to wear that outfit at some point during the week.

LAY OUT CLOTHES THE NIGHT BEFORE

This is very simple to do and will save lots of stress. As I have mentioned numerous times, your morning will be the craziest time of the day. Laying out your children's clothes the night before (and your own too) will save time and stress the next day. When my husband is getting the kids ready for the bath, before I jump in the shower, I do my quick "run through." First I gather up all the dirty clothes they have taken off and dump them in the hamper. Next I go into each room and 1) put their shoes away, 2) get clothes for the next day, and lay them out on bathroom floor, and 3) get diaper/pull-up and pajamas for the night. Finally I head back to the bathroom to drop off PJ's before I jump in the shower. This entire "run through" takes me about five minutes but greatly reduces the mess and time it takes to get out of the house in the morning. This is definitely something you want to work into your daily routine.

BATHE CHILDREN TOGETHER

For as long as they like it and you can fit them in the same tub, bathe your children together. This will save you a lot of time and hopefully make the event much more fun, as children love to play together. It also helps limit any fear a child may have as they see their sister or brother going through the same cleansing ritual. Be sure to have age-appropriate toys in the tub and give them time to play as they will dread bath time if you don't. When you introduce a new child to the routine, make sure you talk to the older children about what is allowed and not allowed. There may be some resentment that they can't splash anymore, so talk to them ahead of time and let them know all the fun stuff they can still do in the bath. Some of the best (and worst) moments with our children have been in the bath. I can vividly remember when Ben made Claire laugh for the first time while taking a bath. Now Sarah is about to join the fun, and I am sure we will have many more Kodak moments.

As your children get older, you can start to allow them to shower with you. This allows them to transition to a shower in a safe environment because they are with Mom or Dad. We have begun to do this with Ben (age three-and-a-half) and Claire (age two), which has saved me a lot of time as I can get all three of us showered in less than fifteen minutes, allowing us more time to read and play at night.

HANGING CLOTHES VERSUS DRAWER STORAGE

This one may seem a bit confusing to many of you as it takes time to hang clothes, so it may feel like an extra step. While that is true, the amount of time it will save you in the end is worth the extra few minutes up front. Specifically, I have found three key benefits to hanging my children's clothes in an armoire or closet versus putting them in drawers:

1. **Easier to see size of clothing**. When you hang up clothes it is very easy to access the tags on the clothes to see the size. When your children are infant/toddler age, the sizes change so frequently it is important to be able to see the sizes on the tags. In addition, every brand's sizes run differently. OshKosh may run big while Carter's may run small. By hanging the clothes up you can visually see how large they are, in addition to the actual size on the tag, and use this to help guide what fits when.

2. **Easier to locate clothes**. Drawers are easy to just throw things in, which is the problem. You throw things in, and then you can't see what is what and have to rely on your over-stretched memory to remember what you have, what it looks like, what it goes with, etc. When you hang up the clothes, you hang outfits together, and you can see the entire garment which makes it easier to find long sleeves versus short, the three pieces that go together, and so on.

3. **Wardrobe rotation**. Okay, so I am a type A personality who likes to make sure my children don't wear the same clothes in the same week (or two ☺). When you hang up the clothes always hang the newly washed (and hence latest worn) clothes on the right-hand side, so when you search for something to wear you look to the left. This also insures you don't forget an outfit, and you use all the great gifts you are given. With my first child, I relied more on drawers and found many outfits buried near the bottom that he never had a chance to wear as he had outgrown them by

the time I found them. Hanging clothes helps minimize this oversight.

In the end, hanging clothes makes it easier to find the right outfit at the right time. It also gives you a sense of how many and what type of items you have already. As the child grows, this system works as a visual inventory to help guide what additional pieces need to be purchased.

CLAIRE'S CLOSET

BE PRODUCTIVE DURING BABY'S NAPS

This tip is really only applicable for those of you with one child at home. Every child is different and it often takes a while (months) to settle into a true nap schedule. The key for you is to utilize every nap in some way, regardless of whether it is a short cat nap of twenty minutes or a three-hour nap. Most doctors agree the best thing you could do is sleep yourself. Personally, I have never really been able to do this. Given that I couldn't fall asleep and managed enough sleep at night, I used the naps for household tasks and to write this book. On all my maternity leaves my key goal for our household was to make weekends leisurely and full of family time. Given that I was home all week, I had time to do all the stuff I normally had reserved for weekends when I was working. I used naptime to finish the errands and work around the house.

Let's start with shorter naps and some suggestions for what to get done. With every nap, there is the awkward five minutes in the beginning when you don't really know if the child has fallen asleep or not. During this time you can make your bed; unload the dishwasher; throw in a load of laundry; write in the baby book, first-year calendar or journal if you keep one; brush your teeth; wash your face, put makeup on, or get dressed.

Once you know the baby is asleep you can do more lengthy tasks like fold and put away the laundry, prepare a meal, vacuum (be sure you are not that close to baby's room), check your e-mail, download photos to a Web site, put photos away in scrap books, and so on. When I knew the baby was down for a good nap, I tried to tackle some big projects I had on my list including painting a room or writing tips in my book.

MULTIPLE BABYSITTERS TO CHOOSE FROM

While you may want to use the same babysitter all the time, so your children are comfortable with this person, this is usually not possible. Most teenagers or college students are very busy and getting time on their calendars can be very difficult. This is why it is really important that you have a group of babysitters—ideally three or four—to choose from. Don't always call the same one as your first choice. Alternate to give them business and keep the kids comfortable with each one. If you prefer to use the same sitter each time, try to put her on "retainer" and agree that you will use her each Saturday night (or Friday) at the same time. Even in this case it is good to have backups whom the kids know just in case your normal sitter isn't available due to an unusual circumstance (like a family wedding).

We have found fifteen to twenty to be the perfect age for sitters. Once we had three kids we went toward the high end of the scale. Given how close in age they are, they may be a lot for a fifteen-year-old to handle. However, if you have children who are a bit older or only have one child, I would recommend finding a fourteen- or fifteen-year-old you like, because after they hit driving age it becomes *a lot* harder to get them to sit on a weekend night. If you know any teachers or administrators at the local high school they may be able to refer you to potential sitters. The other great pool to find sitters in is college students. They always need money and have a social life every night, so Friday and Saturday nights aren't as precious as they are to high school students. Many colleges or universities have education programs where you can post ads for sitters.

BREAST-FEED

In addition to the fact that research supports breast milk as the best source of nutrition for your baby, it is by far the easiest feeding choice and saves you a ton of time. Think about it, you are never without food. No dashes to the store to buy formula, no mixing, heating or reheating formula, no washing of bottles, worrying if you have enough food or bottles with you, calculating how much you will need on your weeklong vacation, etc. As you try to get yourself or your family ready to leave the house, the less you have to worry about the better.

Even better, by breast-feeding you can feed the baby anywhere. You aren't tied down by the ability to heat up the bottle or keep the bottle refrigerated. You would die if I told you all the different places I have nursed my children…the car, the mall, restaurants, friends' houses, the zoo, airplanes, on a hay ride, a boat cruise (in Belgium), and more. As long as you can be discrete (and any blanket covers that) and make the baby comfortable, you are good to go. This simplifies your life immensely while providing the best nutritional start for your baby. What could be better?

HAVE A STOCK OF BREAST MILK ON HAND

If your job requires any sort of travel, it is essential to have some breast milk frozen. This is not always easy to do, as it requires you to pump in addition to feeding the baby which takes time that you typically don't have. Most women I talked to found it best to pump in the morning, when milk production is highest. Experiment and figure out what time works best for you and try to pump at least a few times a week to build up some stock for:

- When you travel—If your job requires you to travel, you will need to have stock.

- When you go back to work—When you go back to work and begin to pump every few hours instead of actually feeding the baby, your milk production will decline. However, the baby still requires the same amount. The stock of breast milk you created will allow you to stretch the length of time your children will have breast milk instead of formula.

- When you go out—Whether you go out with your husband or friends, you can't feed your child if she's not with you. Having stock allows the sitter to give the baby a bottle of breast milk.

- If you get sick—Many antibiotics can not be taken if you are breast-feeding. Typically a physician will try a medicine that is fine for the baby. But if it doesn't work, and your health becomes a bigger issue, you many need to stop breast-feeding while on the medication.

LIMIT THE "AWAKE" TIME DURING NIGHT FEEDINGS

I have been thinking about this one a lot lately with Sarah just turning seven weeks old as I write this. When I had Ben, our night feedings were a bit different than they are today with Sarah. I would feed him in bed with me, then get up and go into the bathroom where I would change his diaper. The light often woke him up a bit, which meant I then had to rock him to sleep, which took time. On average I was awake for forty minutes. This was getting very exhausting. I told my friend Tuija (from my Brussels baby group), and she suggested that I not change his diaper at every feeding. She began to do this with her daughter Tuuli, and it helped reduce the amount of awake time. This worked perfectly, allowing Ben to go back to sleep very quickly without the movement and light from the changing process. For the times you do have to change the baby's diaper, try to limit the amount you move the baby around. For example, if you feed him in bed, change him in bed.

With Claire and Sarah, I set up a diaper station in my bedside-table drawer. Their cradle was beside my bed so this was a close location. When Sarah wakes up I first change her diaper, which tends to wake her up so she feeds better. Additionally, feeding the baby often puts the baby to sleep or into a more sedate state so you don't want to wake her by changing her afterward. After the first breast I make sure I burp her before I give her the second breast. Sometimes she falls asleep and doesn't want it, but usually the burping keeps her awake. After the second breast, I try to burp her again, but usually she is fast asleep. On average we are awake about twenty minutes from beginning to end. With a newborn up three times a night the maximum amount of awake time for me is about an hour. I never really leave my bed, and the lights are off (I have a nightlight by the cradle) so I feel like I am "resting" during the feeding, which makes it easier for me to fall back asleep.

DON'T BE AFRAID TO ASK FOR HELP

If you are a working mother, you are a very busy lady. Regardless of how organized and efficient you are, there are times when you simply need some help. It could be as easy as picking up a child from an event or as difficult as having a family member travel a distance to watch the kids for an extended stay while you take a well-deserved vacation with your husband. Regardless of the magnitude, don't be afraid to ask for help. Family and friends often want to help, particularly when a new baby arrives. They are simply waiting for you to ask so not to impose on you at a busy time. You will need to create your "village" that it takes to raise a child. If you don't live near family, use friends and neighbors in place of the more traditional extended family.

It is important that you also extend the same help to others when they need it, particularly if you do not live close to family. Cook the meal for a neighbor when they have a newborn or a sick family member; volunteer to drive a friend's child to the game when you know her spouse is traveling for work; have a neighbor's child over for a sleepover so they don't have to get a sitter. Each time you offer this type of assistance it will likely travel full circle and help you when you are in a bind in the future. Remember to not let your pride stand in the way: Simply ask for the help as most people won't offer help until they know you are comfortable receiving it.

BUY CLOTHES A YEAR AHEAD

Buying children's clothes can either be a lot of fun or a really stress-ful situation. Given how cute they are, I personally think it should be fun. In an effort to enjoy it, save money, and never have to run out at the last minute to buy something, I buy 90 percent of my children's clothes about a year before they will wear them. Children grow at very different rates—sometimes really fast, sometimes not so fast. They may wear their size 2 clothes for a full year but their size 3 for six months. The last thing you want to do is run out and buy clothes at the last minute because they've outgrown everything. Of-ten when you have to do this, you can't find what you need because the store has already gotten rid of their in-season merchandise. To reduce the risk of this happening, I buy in advance.

When stores put their clothes on sale at the end of the season I bulk shop for the next year. For instance, this winter I went to the outlet mall and hit OshKosh, Carter's, and the Children's Place, buying sizes 4T and 2T for my kids who now wear sizes 3 and 18 months respectively. At Target I bought summer pants (in January) for my daughter in size 3T, 4T, and 5T because they were adorable and only $6. How could I resist? I try not to shop for something to wear now, but keep size in mind, particularly if your child is growing at a slower or faster pace than average. Perhaps my kids aren't wearing the latest fashion, but on the positive side I have fun, reduce the amount of shopping I need to do, and save a lot of money.

FAST BREAKFAST THAT CAN BE EATEN ON THE GO

Children need a healthy breakfast to get their day off to the right start. If you have in-home childcare, this isn't an issue because the childcare provider can help prepare the meal. But if your childcare is outside of the home, you will need to find choices that are easy to make and portable. Additionally, you'll want to have a lot of choices on hand to make sure something sounds good as children go through likes and dislikes quicker than gas prices change. Any kind of fruit—a banana, bowl of grapes, sliced apples or pears, strawberries, or a clementine—is a great choice. I like to combine some fruit with a carbohydrate of some sort. Our favorites are muffins (Entenmanns's mini-muffins come in a box of six bags of four muffins), bagels, cinnamon raisin toast, frozen waffles, or French toast. Yogurt is also a good choice once your children are a little older, especially the squeezable yogurt that doesn't require a spoon. Add a cup of juice, and their day is off to a great start in less than five minutes, making the ride to school a little quieter and much happier. On the negative side, your car will be an absolute mess from crumbs and wrappers. I keep wishing someone will invent a car seat that has an easy to remove cover so I could wash it more than a few times a year. Until that happens, my kids will continue to sit on crumbs. ☺

For those who have to prepare lunch, either for daycare or school, be sure to prepare it the evening before to limit the amount of tasks that must be done to get out of the house each morning.

DIAPER STATIONS THROUGHOUT THE HOUSE

I have read that the average newborn can go through up to twelve diapers a day, needing a change about every two hours. By the time a child is around potty-training age (let's say three, which is the early end), he or she is wearing about five diapers per day at a minimum. This means a child will need to be changed over five thousand times in her life. It can be much higher depending on when they begin to sleep through the night and when they are potty trained and wearing underwear.

If you are trying to lose weight, then perhaps this is a good excuse to keep the diaper-changing station only in the nursery. In my world, even if this is the case (which it is, everyone wants to lose their pregnancy pounds), going upstairs for each change is too time-consuming and inefficient. Further, as you have multiple children, it is just not practical to have to leave the area where they are to change a diaper. In our house we now have six areas where we change diapers: 1) great room on main living floor, 2) our bathroom where the children take their baths, 3) nursery, 4) Ben's bedroom, 5) Claire's bedroom, and 6) next to my bed. At every station we have the relevant diaper sizes, wipes, and ointment in a convenient spot.

The great room station is simply a basket (see photo) located under our coffee table. It is very discrete and fits the décor well. At this station we have every diaper size and a changing pad as the surface we change on is the couch. We keep our refill supply in the pantry for easy access to this location. The same is true for our bathroom, in that we have every size diaper to change the kids before or after a bath (our tub is the largest so we bathe there). In the kids' bedrooms we only keep their size diapers, of course. This is for their morning and evening diaper changes as we get them dressed. The floor or bed works perfectly well, depending on the age of the child. All backup diapers are stored in the children's closets or the garage, giving us storage on both floors to limit the time it takes to restock. When you do restock, check all areas at the same time to limit the amount of times you need to do it per week or month.

BEN'S DIAPER STATION

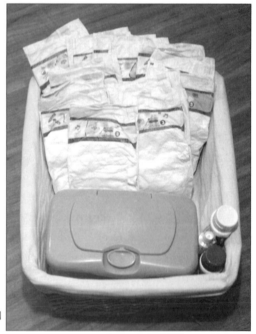

GREAT ROOM STATION

DVR, ON DEMAND, AND VIDEOS

There will be times in your day or week when you need virtually uninterrupted time to accomplish something: make dinner, pay bills, take a shower, or simply decompress. With multiple children, this time is not very easy to find, particularly if your spouse is not around to help. Regardless of what Madonna thinks, I have found that letting my children watch TV or a video is the easiest way to keep them happy, quiet, and preoccupied in a safe environment while I do what I need to. It is important to limit the amount of time each day they watch TV, as it can be addictive for children. It is also important to closely monitor and choose what you allow your children to watch.

We have found DVDs , Kids On Demand (that includes PBS, Nick Jr., and other channels), and a DVR to be the most helpful. DVDs are great because you can choose the story/movie to be sure they are age appropriate. Additionally, if you have a portable player (which I recommend), you can move it anywhere around the house as needed to keep the kids close by (it can also be used on planes, vacation, and more). Our favorite infant and toddler DVDs are the *Baby Einstein* collection; we have them all and can say they helped teach our kids many things from colors to shapes to animals to words. *Little Einstein* is now a favorite for our preschooler. We also love *Sesame Street*, *Wiggles*, *Dragon Tales*, *Thomas the Tank Engine*, and *Jo-Jo's Circus* DVDs as well. For long trips in the car we allow our kids to watch their DVDs, which makes traveling much easier and less stressful.

Another helpful invention for busy homes is the Digital Video Recorder (DVR). If you don't have one, get one. It is the best $10 a month you will spend. We record our kid's favorite shows and allow them to watch one each night before they go to bed, and in the morning while I am getting ready. Now, Playhouse Disney, PBS, and Noggin shows are accessible when we want them, so we never miss a favorite and have saved many episodes.

Also, most cable companies now offer a service called OnDemand. It allows you to watch a selection of stations and shows when you choose versus at their scheduled time. PBS is often offered so your children can now watch *Sesame Street*, *Arthur*, or *Dragon Tales* at any time of the day. Be sure to check your cable companies offerings and sign up for the service if it is available as educational children's shows are hard to find after 6 P.M.

A couple of other good sources for DVDs are your local library and Ebay. At the library you can check out videos for one to two weeks, depending on the title, and often renew them online if necessary. This offers a wide variety for your child at no cost to you. A co-worker of mine, Teresa, buys most of her DVDs used on Ebay. This is very cost effective, and with so many people selling on Ebay there is always a terrific selection to choose from.

HAVE INFANT CLOTHES
READY BEFORE BABY ARRIVES

This is a no-brainer tip, but when you are busy running after and taking care of a toddler or preschooler, sometimes you simply forget. Take a weekend afternoon to sort through the infant clothes, wash them, and get them into drawers or a closet before the baby is due. Given that all of my children arrived early, I would recommend planning this a month before the due date just to be sure. If it is your first child, wash some of the clothes you received as gifts and put them away. *Do not* wash every gift you get as you will find you don't need all fifteen onesies you received. Wash enough for the first few weeks, and then see how often you are washing clothes, before washing or exchanging the remaining gifts.

As you get the clothes ready, survey the amount you have in each size. I have found that you do not need as many of the 0-3 month clothes that you receive as gifts. If your child will be born in warmer months they are more comfortable in onesies, sleepers, and comfy clothes. They don't want to be in dresses, sweaters, shirts, or fancy clothes. Despite how adorable they are, exchange the fancier outfits for a larger size so they can actually use them—you won't have to feel guilty when you put them into the storage box with the tags still on them.

JOIN OR START A BABY GROUP

If you are a working mom it is not easy to "fall into" the stay-at-home-mom activities and groups. Even if a neighbor or friend is kind enough to invite you to join an existing group, often you feel like an outsider looking in, given your limited time at home. But don't give up hope, and don't fear that you will spend your entire leave home alone with your new bundle of joy (not that that is a horrible situation, but we all need to get out every now and then). Instead take things into your own hands and start your own baby group. It is pretty easy to spot women "in your shoes" as their bellies rival yours in size. Start networking at work, in your neighborhood, church, or circle of friends to figure out who will be on leave at the same time as you. Talk about starting a group and agree to get back in touch after the babies are born.

I have started three different groups with each child. After Ben I got together with the women who were in my physiology class in Belgium. We saw each other once a week for the last ten or so weeks of our pregnancy so we couldn't imagine not seeing each other after the babies were born. We started to meet after the last baby was born and continued to meet until I moved back to the U.S. I still keep in touch with the women and look forward to reuniting with them in the future.

With Claire, as I mentioned earlier in the book, there were four other brand managers on my floor who were pregnant at the same time. I was the last one to give birth, after which I invited everyone to my house for lunch. This turned into a weekly gathering with the host preparing a nice lunch for everyone. With Sarah, I sent an e-mail to all my friends who were expecting, asking them if they were interested in forming a group. Of course they were, and we now meet weekly on Wednesday afternoons to have a nice mid-afternoon snack and great conversation. Take some initiative and start the group. You will learn a lot, have a lot of fun, and become even more prepared for the next baby.

TEACH THE CHILDREN TO WORK IT OUT WITH ONE ANOTHER

This tip will not only save you an incredible amount of time but, more importantly, it teaches your children a valuable lesson for later in life. No matter how much you teach your children and how well mannered they are, they will have disputes with their siblings or other children. Typically, these situations end with them or the other child running to you to "tattle." My advice to you is to respond to the tattle with this statement: "Did you use your words and talk to your friend about what they did and how it made you feel?" In other words, go work it out. The worst thing you can do is run to "solve" the situation when they come to you. This makes them dependent on you to solve their problems instead of teaching them how to resolve conflicts, and takes a lot of time (as they tend to happen quite a bit). It can also scare the other children who are involved if an adult is interrogating them about what happened.

Parents today have gotten the nickname of "helicopter parents" for reasons like this: They run to their children in times of trouble rather than teaching their children how to settle issues, become more independent, and use language to talk to someone they are upset with, instead of crying or asking for their parents' help. My hope is that my children and yours will learn to respect others and share their feelings when someone has upset them, and only have to come to their parents in times of true need.

WHEN ALL ELSE FAILS, SING A SONG

There is just something about music that calms and mesmerizes a child. Mobiles, music boxes, Baby Einstein videos, and swings with music are all tools used to soothe babies and capture their attention in a calm way. Music also has the ability to make just about any task or situation fun. When the kids are acting up in the car...sing a song. When your son doesn't want to brush his teeth, make up a song about brushing your teeth. When you head downstairs in the morning, march in a line while singing a song. When you clean up the toys, sing a song. They have all worked for me, despite being officially tone deaf (according to my eighth-grade music teacher).

You can either make up your own song or simply sing any of the fun songs we all grew up with. I have listed some of our favorites below to give you a head start:

- *"If you're happy and you know it, clap your hands..."*
- *"There was a farmer who had a dog, and Bingo was his name-o..."*
- *"Old McDonald had a farm, e-i-e-i-o..."*
- *"This old man, he played one, he played knick-knack..."*
- *"The wheels on the bus go round and round..."*
- *"One, two buckle my shoe..."*
- *"Take me out to the ballgame..."*
- *"Clean up, clean up, everybody everywhere..."*
- *"All around the cobbler's bench the monkey chased the weasel..."*

It's also worthwhile to invest in some great kids' CDs for the long car rides to give you an alternative to videos on long trips and to aid in your singing for the short ones. Our favorites are the Laurie Berkner Band, *Baby Einstein* series, and *102 Full Length Children's Songs* by Twin Sisters. Ask friends and your daycare provider for their suggestions as well.

LIMIT YOUR CHILDREN'S ACTIVITIES

The easiest way for your life to spin completely out of control is to feel the need to enroll your children in every activity available to them. I am not sure what causes this desire. Maybe you read that most of the brain is developed by the age of five and want to expose your children to as much as possible to help it develop. Or maybe it is just "keeping up with the Joneses." Either way, most parents do not feel complete unless their children are in soccer, baseball, ballet, swim lessons, piano lessons—all before kindergarten. My advice to you is—don't succumb to the pressure. Once you start, it is a quick downward spiral, particularly if you have children close in age. You will quickly say goodbye to those precious family dinners and activities together. Instead, say hello to hours standing along a soccer or baseball field, or outside a dance studio (because it is not politically correct to drop children off anymore).

Our personal view is we enroll our children in activities that are important relative to their age, like swim lessons. We felt they should know how to swim at a young age so we enrolled them. When Ben turned five we gave him skating lessons as he has an interest in hockey, and it is easier to develop this skill younger before fear sets in. All other activities will not start until they are older, a minimum of seven, when they understand how to make a choice and will choose which activities are of most interest to them. When it comes to sports, we will teach our children the rules of any game they express an interest in and play with them in our yard or driveway to develop their basic skills. This decision is challenged frequently when every neighborhood kid heads out in their soccer or cheerleading gear. You need to remind yourself of what you have instead and enjoy the great basketball, baseball, football, and hockey games outside with your family and the fond memories they create.

Tips and Time Savers:

For Managing You

*T*his section will provide you with some tips to take better care of yourself. I am sure you are thinking, "Why do I need tips on how to care for myself? I have done it for years." But this was before you had a child of your own, someone who counts on you for everything. It must be part of the hormone changes that come with pregnancy that makes you put your child's needs ahead of your own. This means you have to remind yourself that you still count too. I promise you that you will have a point when you look at yourself in the mirror and say, "What happened?" Unless you consciously make and take time for yourself you will find yourself very exhausted and, depending on the length of your maternity leave, mentally unready for the return to work. I encourage you to take these tips to heart and begin using them. It will make some of the other tips easier to execute.

DON'T COMPARE YOURSELF TO STAY-AT-HOME MOMS

This valuable advice is very hard to follow. It is human nature to compare oneself to others; unfortunately, we often compare ourselves even when there is not a direct comparison to be made. That is the case between stay-at-home and working moms. They both have their challenges and neither job is easy. Additionally, each one thinks the grass is greener on the other side. Stay-at-home moms may be envious of the independence of a working mom and the fact that they get to have adult conversations every day. Working moms are often envious of the additional time spent with the children. Like any major decision in life, there are pros and cons to both situations, and the key is to know yourself and which role is best for you.

For me it was being a working mom. I worked very hard, as did my parents, to pay for my education. More importantly, I absolutely love what I do each and every day. I am happy and fulfilled each day and believe this makes me a better mom because I cherish every waking minute I have with my kids—feeling complete and satisfied emotionally, intellectually, and spiritually. I will also be the first to admit that I am not sure I would make a great stay-at-home mom. It takes a lot of patience (which at times I don't have) and creativity (to figure out how to stimulate a child for ten hours a day), which at times can be hard for my type A, process-oriented personality. I encourage you to make the choice after much consideration and then be comfortable in your own shoes. Of course you can change your mind at any point and either go back to work or choose to stay at home at some point. The key is don't ever try to compare yourself to the other "job" while you are in it. It will only cause unnecssary stress.

FIND A SIMPLE WAY TO INDULGE YOURSELF

Being half of a dual-career couple with kids is not an easy life, especially if you are the female partner. You constantly put other people's needs before your own and are the last person "treated" in the home. But for the household to thrive and prosper, you need to be happy and in control. My tip for you is to find an easy way to indulge or "treat" yourself. Think about what revives you, makes you happy, or relieves your stress. Ask yourself, "If I had two free hours, what would I do with them?" The answer should be your indulgence. Personally, my indulgence is reading *People* magazine cover to cover every Friday night. I look forward to opening the mailbox after a long week of work and seeing who is on the cover. I love pop culture and feeling informed about what is going on, so this is my perfect indulgence. After I put the kids to bed, I jump into my bed and snuggle in with my magazine and just read until the last page is turned—often next to my husband, who reading his indulgence, *Sports Illustrated*.

For many of my friends, their indulgence is something out of the house and often related to beauty: massages, manicures, pedicures, and facials are very popular. Others shop until they drop, always hunting for the latest style or hottest bargain. Others bring fresh flowers into their house each week or go out to eat at their favorite restaurant. These all make the respective person happy and relaxed. The key is to find an indulgence that is simple, easy to do, can be booked in advance, doesn't take a lot of planning, and certainly doesn't cause stress in any way. It should also be something you can do on a regular basis, ideally weekly, as you will need it.

SLEEP, SLEEP, AND MORE SLEEP

It takes a lot of energy to keep up with one child, let alone multiple children. This energy drain on top of a long workweek leads to many exhausted mothers and fathers on the weekends, just in time to run from swimming lessons to the grocery store, soccer game, church, and so on. While you may be able to "survive" on less than the recommended amount of sleep (usually seven hours for a woman) before parenthood, this will be very difficult to do after parenthood. The key is to get sleep. It is that simple. I could survive on seven hours before I got married and had kids, though I preferred eight.

Once I had Ben the minimum I could survive on was eight (10:30 P.M. - 6:30 A.M.); if I got less than that two nights in a row, I was a zombie at work and at home. When I am pregnant I need to increase my night's sleep by one hour, sleeping nine hours each night (9:30 P.M. - 6:30 A.M.) and often ten on Friday nights after the workweek wiped me out. This was very difficult when I was pregnant with Sarah as I had two others to care for, but Arnie knew how exhausted I was and would pick up the slack on Friday nights to keep me happy and healthy. My advice would be to try to get an additional hour after the kids are born to refresh your body each night. The downside to this advice is you probably won't make it to CEO one day (they get on average four to five hours a night), but the upside is you will be more productive each day and feel 100 percent better. ☺

GET A SIMPLE HAIRCUT

Having children does not mean you turn into an "old maid" or stop taking care of yourself. But it does limit the amount of time you have to get ready in the morning. You still need to get to work at a decent hour and many of you need to get your children ready and dropped off before you arrive. Unless you are a morning person or can survive on little sleep, something needs to go in your morning routine. My tip is to get a simple haircut, one that is stylish and cute but requires a little less prep time. Because I only wash my hair every other day to keep it healthy, I like to have a style that can be brought to life on day two as well. Let your stylist know that you want a cut that is easy to style and maintain. Then enjoy your new look.

Note: The photos of me on the cover and back flap were taken May, 2008. At this time I was growing my hair to donate to Pantene's Beautiful Lengths program, in support of the great brand that I am privileged to work on each day. This was the longest I have ever had my hair. It was cut in July and donated.

SHOWER AT NIGHT

Many of you who are reading this in anticipation of having a child may find this hard to believe, but finding time to take a ten-minute shower (uninterrupted) on a regular basis will no longer be a simple task in your life, especially if you have multiple children. Getting out of the house in the mornings is a multi-multi-multi-task project. No matter how much you plan your morning, it is likely that something will go awry. Someone will get up early or late, someone won't want to wear what you have picked out, or you have a bad hair day. Given that most of these situations are out of your control, try to take back some control by showering at night instead of the morning.

Showering at night allows you to shower at a "nonbusy" time, either after the children have gone to bed or while they are in the bath (with your spouse watching them, of course). I have found the most success showering while my husband has our older two in the bath and the baby is happy in her bouncy seat. They get a kick out of the fact that I am washing up at the same time as them (sometimes we race, which helps Dad out), and they like the fact that they can still talk to me. Many times I will simply go to bed with wet hair and style it in the morning so I can help get them in their pajamas, or do my hair after they are in bed. Either way, it still saves at least ten minutes in the morning and endless stress as you know where the kids are, that no one is crying, and you don't have to rush because someone wants you.

ACCESSORIZE ☺

One thing I can promise you is that your body will change with childbirth. You may go back to your pre-pregnancy weight, or even lower than what you originally weighed, but your body will be vastly different. Of course if you work out regularly you can get your original shape back, but I'm guessing that if you have a career and children, you aren't spending as much time at the gym as you used to.

Because your shape is different you will be very frustrated when it comes to your clothing, both during pregnancy and post-pregnancy. Clothes won't fit anymore, and cuts that used to look good don't anymore. You simply don't feel very good in clothes. Like with your hair, you still want to feel good about yourself and look presentable at work. My tip is to fall in love with accessories. Buy the latest trendy shoes, handbags, jewelry, and scarves. It is easy to change your accessories daily to perk up your clothes and out-look. You can also use these accessories while you are pregnant with your next child, making you feel pretty during your higher-weight times. Accessories are also a great gift idea for your husband to buy for you, as he doesn't have to worry about size when shopping for them.

DON'T FORGET ABOUT YOUR HUSBAND

Between morning sickness, sleepless nights, delivery, and breast-feeding, your body takes a huge toll. You are so tired and out of shape, the last thing on your mind is sex. Unfortunately, it is very much on the mind of your husband, as he was counting down until you weren't pregnant. Despite what you may or may not be feeling, make time for your husband. Your marriage or relationship is the most important thing in the household. The best thing you can give your kids is a great relationship with your husband. Take the time to be with your partner, either a date night or a time of the day that is reserved for the two of you. Steal moments whenever you can. Your schedule is hectic and unpredicable, so take these stolen moments when you can instead of waiting for a particular day or time. Surprise each other with little thank yous, gestures, or dates. Hug each other frequently, and remember to tell him you love him each day. There will be a time again when you have those romantic dinners, peaceful evenings, and weekends to yourselves. Until that day comes, force yourself to remember to make time for your partner, and remind him of how the kids were created in the first place. ☺

DON'T OVERCOMMIT

Most dual-career families with children are very good at multitasking as it is required to do the job well. We are used to juggling many balls at once and often get a rush from doing it. It is very important, however, to not overcommit yourself at work, home, or in the community. To keep this from happening, sit down and figure out how much time you have to "give" to others, including your children. How many evenings a week can you be out of the home, either at children's events, games/practices, and community or work activities? Do not book yourself seven nights a week as you will need some evenings to take care of household matters and simply to revive yourself. When you do commit to a group or activity, ensure you fully understand the time commitment involved. How many meetings a month will a not-for-profit board take? How many dinners will a work project take? How many nights will your child's team practice and at what times?

I truly believe that many problems with our society today stem from the fact that we can't simply sit down and relax anymore. We feel if we aren't on the go at all times, or our children aren't enrolled in every sport or activity, then we are selling ourselves short in some way. This leads to our children not being able to sit quietly in one place and constantly being distracted or "bored." It also minimizes the "family" time in the home, moments that are essential to establish family values, morals, memories, and more. Remember that quality and not quantity usually wins out in most situations. Choose the activities for yourself and your family wisely and resist the urge to overcommit simply because you can.

GET THE BABYSITTER THIRTY MINUTES EARLY

The best five dollars you can spend is getting the babysitter to come thirty minutes before you need to leave the house. When you do this, instead of trying to get dressed and ready with three little ones watching and longing for the last few minutes of your attention, you can get ready in peace while the sitter entertains the troops. It also gives you the time to write down the instructions for the sitter to have something to refer to. This is much simpler than delivering a five-minute rundown of who eats what when, bedtimes, pajamas, TV rules, and more. Having the sitter arrive early also gives you the flexibility to get out of the house on time. Often the kids aren't happy that you are leaving, so having the sitter arrive early gives you time to work through the temper tantrums and still not be late for your event.

RUN AWAY FROM HOME TO RECHARGE

There will come a time in every mother's life where she simply needs to recharge her batteries. For some it may come in your child's first year, for others much later, but it will come. When that moment comes, or ideally a few months before you hit the wall, plan a weekend getaway to recharge the batteries. Call your mom, sister, or long-lost best friend and book a get-away weekend. It can be to visit them or to a great spa where you can relax, or even to a hotel downtown. Just make sure it is away from your home (even if you can ship your husband and kids away, being home is too tempting to do chores and such). If you can swing it, run away with your husband at the same time, because often you need some private time.

My first "run away" experience was when my third child turned nine months. Arnie had just turned 40, and it was a good excuse for the two of us to get away. We talked to lots of friends with kids and asked them about their first trip without the kids. They all said a week is too long, because after four or five days you are so sad without the kids, so we decided to do a four-night, five-day all-inclusive trip to Jamaica through Sandals. We flew my parents in from New York to watch the kids, and off we went. While I was sad to leave Sarah so young, after three kids in three years I needed, and my marriage needed, a break from it all.

We had such a great time we decided to make it an annual event for ourselves. This year a good friend got married in Mexico, so it was the perfect excuse to take our annual get-away trip. We keep them to no more than four nights away, to make it easy to get either of our parents to come to watch the kids. Take advantage of these trips to indulge yourselves. Go to the spa, get massages, facials, and so on. If you like to exercise, take advantage of the extra free time. We love to golf so we always try to fit in a round while we are away. Your body, mind, and spirit will be so much better off after time for yourself, and you will have more energy, desire, and love for your family and job.

START A GIRLS' NIGHT OUT

After you have children it is so hard to keep up with girlfriends as they are often in the same boat as you—overworked and tired all the time. Just as you enjoyed starting a baby group when you were on leave, take the initiative to start a girls' night out after you return to work. When I was in Europe I did this with the moms from my baby group. About once every four to six weeks we all went out for dinner together and our husbands watched the kids. While we enjoyed our weekly coffees or walks, it was so nice to have a conversation over a great dinner without infants to care for and toddlers running around. You could also do a girls' night in or a book club—just be sure that no kids are present. Order in food rather than prepare it, rotate houses so the same person doesn't have the stress of cleaning all the time, and create an environment where great conversation can flow. With e-mail it is easy to plan, communicate, and take turns choosing the restaurant or book, and makes it all the more fun.

GIVE YOURSELF A NIGHT OFF

Weekend evenings can become quite exhausting when you have young children—preparing dinner, cleaning up afterwards, bathing the children, preparing for the next day—and that assumes you don't have any activities to go to or errands to run. Every now and then give yourself a night off. Also, be sure your husband also takes a night off every now and then. One way of doing this is to simply have your husband takes the kids out to eat. This gives you peaceful downtime in your home where you can relax in its comfort: take a bath, snuggle in a chair and read a book, call an old friend on the phone, play on the Internet, or simply watch your favorite TV show without interruption. Another way is to leave the house. Go out shopping or to dinner with a friend, sit in a coffee shop and read a book, or go for a workout. Be sure to balance the nights off between you and your spouse, and you will both find you are grateful and less stressed because of it.

TAKE TIME TO EXERCISE

While breast-feeding is the best diet God ever created, it is important to make the time to exercise after you give birth. Your body has just gone through major trauma and is often longing for some attention after nine months of carrying extra weight and working overtime. The easiest way to take care of you is to go for long walks with the baby. Start a walking group with other new moms or neighbors who want to exercise. Many local moms' groups do "mall walking" at the local mall, and many recreation centers offer walking groups. Check your local online support sites to learn more.

My friend Kristen joined *Stroller Fit* in Cincinnati after she had her daughter. *Stroller Fit* is an exercise program that incorporates your baby's stroller into the routines. It can be done indoors in a gymnasium or outside at a park. It is quite a workout and a great way to meet other new moms, and you never have to leave your baby. Check online to see if there is a *Stroller Fit* in your hometown.

Personally, I found it fairly easy to find time to exercise while I was on maternity leave. This allowed me to lose the weight I had gained and feel physically strong when I returned to work. Unfortunately, after I returned to work, and after three children, I now find it almost impossible to find time to exercise regularly. If anyone has any good tips on how to fit it in, I would love to hear from you.

Tips and Time Savers:

For Managing Your Career

This section will help you keep in check the other half of your life that can often consume more than 50 percent of your awake time each week—your career. Whether you work part-time or full-time, first shift or second shift, hourly or salary, it is critical that you set some clear parameters for what you will or can do and what you won't or can't do for your job. This section will give you some tips on how to better manage your boss and subordinates, which will pay dividends to you and your ability to have a fulfilling career and home life.

GET A BLACKBERRY

Given that the nickname for a BlackBerry is "crackberry," you may be asking how this can help you manage your career versus your career managing you. A BlackBerry (Palm, Smartphone, or any other brand) gives you more flexibility with your workday by giving you e-mail access in the palm of your hand. Additionally, you're no longer reliant on your laptop for e-mail. No more lugging it home or on short business trips. You can quickly get updates on key projects, delete spam mail, respond to a request, or send a long-lost friend a quick hello.

I didn't have a BlackBerry until I had my second child. When I was preparing for my leave, HR asked me if there was anything they could do to make my leave easier, given that I would return to the same job. I told them having a BlackBerry would make things easier. I could "stay in touch" and clean out my e-mail easily while managing my baby at home. This was truly a lifesaver for me. While it was very hard to go back to work after four months of the business having no brand manager, I believe having my BlackBerry made it a more pleasant experience and certainly made my leave more enjoyable for me.

The key is not to get addicted to it. If you find yourself doing e-mail for two hours each night with your BlackBerry when you didn't do this before you had it, then something is wrong. It shouldn't add hours to your day. Instead, it should give you some freedom to be productive at times when you couldn't be before: while waiting to present your topic at a meeting; waiting for your plane to arrive/depart; waiting for an appointment (e.g., doctor, haircut); on Sunday night to clean out junk mail so Monday morning is a bit easier; while on your pumping break at work (this is true and was very helpful); between meetings off-site.

... THINK OF YOUR CAREER AS A RACE

Most working moms tend to have some Type A personality in them somewhere. You have made a big choice to have a career, and it is obviously important to you as you have maintained it after having children. This makes it very easy to get pulled into the rat race, the obsession with advancement, of corporate America, civil-working America, or private enterprise. Regardless of how big or small your employer, we all tend to judge ourselves on how we did this year versus last, or versus our peers. Are we making more money? Did we get promoted? Do we have more responsibility? It is very easy to want to stay in the fast-forward career world. The key is to think of your career as a marathon rather than a sprint.

You need to look at your career long term. Start with what you want to achieve before you retire. Then think about the next year in terms of what you want to learn and experience rather than what you want to achieve. Make choices about your assignments based upon your life goals and not only your career goals, because the balance is important.

Let me illustrate through a personal story. In the fall of 2004 I was told I was ready for my second promotion at P&G. While I was thrilled to receive the positive feedback and vote of confidence, I also knew that I wanted another baby (Claire was around eight months old). Arnie and I made the decision that I would rather delay my promotion and take an extended maternity leave while I was "in between assignments" rather than take the promotion immediately and have to return to the same job after a shorter maternity leave. I had done the latter with Claire and never felt I was completely at home with her as my mind was also wrapped around work.

I could make this decision because I didn't think of my career as a race. I don't measure it with regard to a level or salary, but instead by how much it challenges and stretches me. If you think of your career as a race to get to a certain level, you will constantly be torn between your family and work, never feeling comfortable with how you are performing in either area. This adds a lot of stress to your life and makes your household a tense environment, which is unhealthy for everyone living in it.

KNOW YOUR BENEFITS ☺

This is one near and dear to me as I have made *sooooo* many mistakes regarding my benefits it is embarrassing. Most Fortune 500 companies, and certainly every Fortune 50 company, publish documents that outline the key elements of their benefit programs like maternity leaves, vacation time, healthcare, and retirement plans. If having a family is important to you, be sure to research these benefits before you interview for a job, as they are the most important for a dual-career household. Another great place to look is in publications that rank companies in how they perform regarding "women's issues" like childcare, maternity leave, and career advancement. Each year *Working Mother* publishes a list of their top one hundred companies to work for. In addition, there is a more general best-places-to-work list compiled by *Fortune* for the men reading this book. Read these lists before you make your final decision. While the company you are considering doesn't have to be on the list, you should at least know how it fares on the criteria used to conduct the rankings.

Before accepting a position or having your first child, be sure you know the company's policy regarding:

1. Maternity leave of absence—By law any company employing more than twenty-five persons has to give twelve weeks maternity leave of absence under the Family Medical Leave Act (also good for elder care or care of a family member. Specifics on FMLA and Pregnancy Discrimination Act can be found in Appendix F). In most states this leave does not have to be paid, and begins when you leave work. Hence if you are put on bed rest before the delivery, the clock starts ticking and reduces the amount of time at home after the birth of your child. When interviewing or doing research be sure to find out the policy regarding maternity leave, specifically: a) how long can you take off and be guaranteed your job, b) how long is paid leave, c) how is the leave paid (for example, through disability insurance, etc.), d) what is the cost to you to have coverage for a paid leave (at P&G

it is paid through short-term disability insurance), e) will they hold your same position for a period of time, or do you have to come back to a new position?

2. **Health Plans**—Make sure you understand the health insurance the company offers, specifically: a) type of plans (HMO versus choice plans), b) premium costs; c) out-of-pocket costs; d) coverage for adoption and fertility treatments, and e) what happens to your insurance when you take a childcare leave of absence.

3. **Childcare**—Many larger companies provide daycare services. These can be on- or off-site, subsidized or not subsidized. Research what your company offers with regard to childcare including; a) location, b) cost, and c) philosophy.

4. **Retirement Programs**—There are many different types of retirement programs in corporate America, and I am not a financial expert so I won't try to explain them. What is critical for you to know is what investment the company makes regarding your retirement, specifically: a) Is it funded by the company or personally? b) Do they have a matching program for a 401K? c) How much as a percentage of salary do they put into retirement (if company funded)? d) If stock related, what has the performance been over the past twenty years with regard to appreciation?

It can be very confusing at times as often your benefits will change year to year. Don't be afraid to ask human resources, your office manager, or a colleague for assistance. It is very easy to make a mistake that can cost you hundreds or thousands of dollars, so take the time. Unfortunately, this happened to me (and Arnie, I guess, but it was my mistake). I took an extended leave after my first child, hence I wasn't getting paid after the first eight weeks. Somehow during my extended leave I missed an e-mail to re-enroll in disability. To make a long story short, when I got pregnant again and called to say I was going out on short-term disability, I was told by our employee service center that I didn't have coverage, costing me two months pay. Know your benefits inside and out!

TO KNOW YOUR BOSS AND EACH OTHERS' EXPECTATIONS

When you start a new role or have a new boss in your current role, it is very important to get to know each other's styles and expectations. What do they expect you to deliver? What do they expect you to report to them on? What decisions can you make autonomously and what decisions require their input or approvals? In addition, it is very important that the person you work for understand what hours you are accessible for meetings and phone calls. While you may be uneasy saying that you are not available for meetings before 8:00 A.M., if your personal situation does not allow that, it is perfectly fine for you to request that from your boss, or offer to have a meeting by phone from home.

I like to have a very informal meeting first to get to know one another–to understand their background, family, personal passions, and more…what makes them tick. Make sure they understand the same about you. I also share what I think makes a strong working relationship (trust, honesty, coaching/feedback) versus a weak relationship (no trust, competitive, no ownership) so we can try to build a strong relationship from the start.

We all think and work in different ways and are driven by different goals, so it is critical to get on the same page early in the relationship. Understand where differences exist so you can manage them and utilize them rather than try to diminish them. Everyone will be happier for it.

SET EXPECTATIONS
WITH YOUR DIRECT REPORTS

Every manager is different with regard to how they like to work, how much autonomy they give to their subordinates, how they like to give feedback, and so on. In order to ensure you and your subordinates are on the same page, I recommend having a very informal meeting first to get to know one another—to understand their background, family, personal passions and more…what makes them tick. Make sure they understand the same about you. I like to explain my management and coaching styles. I also share what I think makes a strong working relationship (trust, honesty, coaching/feedback) versus a weak relationship (no trust, competitive, no ownership) so we can try to build a strong relationship from the start.

After the initial meeting I recommend having a more formal on-boarding to go over the specific work the individual will be doing. For each project, discuss your expectations regarding what the subordinate will deliver. In this meeting you should also talk about what the subordinate can expect from you regarding weekly one-on-one meetings, coaching, feedback, and support. It is important to let your direct reports know what you expect regarding timing of the deliverables and lead time to read any document in advance of it being forwarded on or shared. I feel very uncomfortable having to make a decision without the proper information or lead time, so I stress this concern to my subordinates. It is also very important that you understand how they like to work, when and how they like to get feedback (immediately following the meeting or in our one-on-one, oral or written, positive and negative) and their expectations of you.

SET PARAMETERS FOR WORK REGARDING HOURS AND TRAVEL

This is absolutely essential for you to be able to succeed in managing a dual-career household with children. You need to be very clear with yourself, your boss, and your partners at work regarding what hours are acceptable for work and how much you are willing to travel. Let's take one at a time. For work hours you need to be somewhat flexible, as crises erupt and you need to deal with them. Determine with your husband what your typical day will look like, who will drop off the kids, and who will pick up the kids. This plan will set your typical day. I set my typical work hours as 8:30 A.M.-6:00 P.M. Regardless of whether I am picking up or dropping off the kids, I can be at work during these hours. If I am needed for a meeting earlier or later than these hours, my assistant needs to check with me prior to booking the meeting to ensure I can make it and that my husband can take care of the children. My partners (agency, cross-functional, peers), subordinates, and boss know this and work with her accordingly. The most important thing is that whoever "owns" your calendar (the person who is allowed to book meetings and change meetings) knows your hours and plans with them in mind.

For travel, if you only wish to travel a certain amount per week, month, or quarter you need to make this clear. If your family limits the amount you can travel, it is essential that you discuss this with your boss so you can ensure you are put in positions that can accommodate it. If you need to be in town every Monday because you are the Brownie troop leader, then it should be blocked on your calendar. If your job requires you to attend a meeting out of town each quarter, then book it well in advance and clear your home calendar so there are no last-minute issues regarding the kids or personal matters. Be open, upfront, and flexible and you should be able to manage a certain amount of travel even with a bustling household.

PRACTICE THE 80/20 RULE

This is a really important tip to follow. If you are anything like me, or a lot of the working women I know, you are a perfectionist. You like to plan things well in advance, to dot every *i* and cross every *t*, and never do anything halfway. Early in my career I would stay an extra hour or two to make sure my documents were perfect before a review with my boss, even though I knew my boss would have lots of changes and builds simply because she was more experienced and knowledgeable than I was.

When you have children, not only can you not afford to put in extra time to edit documents and make non-value-added changes, with time you realize it just isn't worth it. As you advance in your career you come to realize what is "good enough" or "80 for the 20," as others say. If you know your objectives and what is expected of you, it is much easier to practice the 80/20 rule. Learn to recognize when your work is good enough to share with others, or when you are adding value and when you aren't, or which meetings you should attend and which you shouldn't. All of these are examples of practicing the 80/20 rule, getting 80 percent of the results with 20 percent of the effort. It is truly amazing how much time we spend trying to get it to 100 percent. I have found I am so much more efficient since I actively began to put this rule into practice.

The easiest way to start putting the 80/20 rule into practice is to simply ask yourself, "Is this adding value?" every time you sit down to do something. If you cannot with full confidence say "yes" or that your boss would not say "yes," then don't do the work. Instead, focus on the tasks that can add value without as much effort, and you will be more productive and less stressed.

COORDINATE CALENDARS WITH YOUR SPOUSE

An electronic calendar is a valuable piece of technology. Not only does it allow other people to see my calendar and book the time they need, but it also allows my husband and I to coordinate our calendars with regards to the children. We have it easy because we both work for the same company and hence have the same calendar software. He and I, along with our assistants, have viewing and writing access to each others' calendars. Any time either of us books an early meeting, a late meeting, or travel, it is entered in the other's calendar, and the time is blocked off to ensure someone is able to drop off, pick up, or be home with the children.

If you do not have the same software as your spouse or access to his calendar, you have two choices. Google, Yahoo, and others now offer calendar services where you and another person (your spouse) can have access and writing privileges to the same calendar. This is the best solution as you can always view the calendar from work or from home when booking an appointment. If you aren't computer people, the second option is to spend five minutes each evening coordinating your calendars to review any early meetings, late meetings, dinner meetings, or travel dates. It is critical that you don't finalize any of these meetings until you have had this review with your spouse. Simply "pencil them in" to block the time but do not confirm until you know your spouse is fine with it. This routine will come in very handy when you book weekend events, vacations, and other activities, as you will be used to reviewing the calendar and blocking time in advance for important events.

HAVE A BACKUP CHILDCARE PLAN

No matter how great your childcare provider is, there will be times when you need a backup plan regarding who will take care of the kids. For example:

- The nanny or au pair is sick
- Your child is sick and cannot go to daycare (most have strict health guidelines)
- The nanny or au pair is on vacation
- The nanny or au pair has a personal emergency

All of these reasons, and many more, would require you to find someone else to care for your children. There are two ways of handling this situation. The first is a "we'll cross that bridge when we get to it" approach, which requires a lot of flexibility on your part as you are assuming either you or your husband can watch the kids if the situation arises. This approach requires a job that allows you to work remotely.

The second approach is securing a backup plan. If your child tends to pick up the virus going around more often than not, or your job does not allow for flexibility (no sick days, can't work remotely), this is the option for you. There are childcare services in most metropolitan areas that you can join by paying a fee to belong. Once you are a member you can call on the service to provide last-minute help when needed. The hourly rate is often higher than average as the providers are older and more experienced than your average sitter, but it provides peace of mind and security as you know your child will be well cared for, no matter the situation.

KNOW WHEN TO CALL IN HELP FOR WHEN YOU TRAVEL

It is important to know how long you and your husband feel comfortable being a "single parent" when the other travels, and at what point it becomes too much to handle. Arnie and I have learned through trial and error that a trip that is any longer than two and-a-half days, or five "shifts" with the kids, is enough to call for help. First let me explain what I mean by a "shift." For working parents, the most difficult times of day are getting out of the house in the morning and the evening routine of cooking dinner, feeding the kids, baths, and bedtime. In our home we call each of these a "shift." So when we look at our travel plans, the first thing we calculate is how many "shifts" the other person will have by themselves. If it is more than five, we then call either one of our parents to see if they can help. For shorter trips (like three days and three nights away) we call Arnie's parents who are closer in Detroit and can drive down.

When I have to do international travel for my job, I plan my trips months in advance. I am gone a minimum of five nights and five days, which always require some extra help. I plan these trips around when my parents visit Cincinnati. For example, every September my parents come for two weeks to celebrate Ben and Sarah's birthdays and spend time with us. When I moved into my current role that requires international travel, I began booking one of my annual trips the second week they are here. This way Arnie has extra help around the house. When we do ask my parents to come at times they were not planning to visit Cincinnati, we always pay their air fare so that it's not a financial burden on them.

The key is to know how long you are comfortable being a single parent. As the kids get older we are finding we can handle more "shifts" than we used to. Like anything that involves children, be flexible, and don't be afraid to ask for some help.

TRY NOT TO TRAVEL AT THE SAME TIME AS YOUR SPOUSE

No matter how well planned your trips and the care of your children are, the only thing for certain is it won't go as planned. A flight is delayed or cancelled, bad weather on either end of your travel, or other factors can cause stress in any situation. But when you and your spouse are both traveling at the same time, this can cause an incredible amount of stress. Once Arnie and I where both traveling at the same time, with an eleven-hour period where we would both be outside of Cincinnati. The plan was I would drop the kids off in the morning before boarding my plane. A sitter would then pick them up from daycare that evening, bring them home, and feed them. Arnie would then arrive home around 8:30 P.M. to relieve the sitter. As you can imagine, that is not how the day turned out. St. Louis (where Arnie was) got hit with a snow storm that shut the airport down (and it was only December 1). Arnie was forced to drive to Cincinnati, arriving at 10 P.M. instead of 8:30 P.M. This was not the end of the world, as our sitter lived in the neighborhood and was a college student more than capable of taking care of the children. But we were still very stressed the entire day, on the phone non-stop concerned about Arnie's drive as well as the children.

We would recommend getting the calendars out in advance and planning your trips so they don't overlap. You will have less stress and sleep easier because of it.

TAKE YOUR VACATIONS

I am amazed by how many Americans don't take their vacation days each year. They end up "selling" them back to their company if they can or simply losing them over time. Your body is an amazing machine at times, but every machine needs a rest every now and then. You need to recharge yourself, in addition to spending quality time with your family. Make sure you treat your vacation as a precious gift that should be enjoyed. Plan them well in advance, try to spread them out throughout the year, and absolutely limit the amount of work done while on vacation. Don't plan to take them during a busy season that will require you to stay in touch and take the computer. Think of the downtimes throughout the year, and try to take them during these times as it will allow you to enjoy them much more.

Over time you may find you need a vacation "in your home." Despite all the best intentions and planning, often the house just takes over. You may need to take some days simply to get things back in order and to let the kids enjoy their home environment. There is nothing wrong with this idea, but I do suggest planning some fun activities to make the time seem special to all of you, even if you just spend the time in your backyard. Of course, eventually your vacations will by default need to coincide with school vacations. Until then, enjoy your freedom, and plan away!

DON'T LIVE TO WORK, WORK TO LIVE

I learned this phrase while on assignment in Belgium. Our European counterparts would always tell Arnie and me, "The problem with Americans is you live to work; in Europe we work to live." What they meant is they work so they can make money, which they can use to enjoy life and their passions—travel, spending time with family, and so on. In the U.S. we often put our careers first and don't spend time on our personal passions. Instead, we spend our income on material goods—a bigger house, a fancier car, or the latest gadget. We measure ourselves by how much we have rather than how much we have experienced or seen. Personally, I think the Europeans have it right and that every dual-career household with children would be better off to remember to live a little.

DON'T BE AFRAID TO ASK

I work for a very large company (over 135,000 employees, $80 billion in sales, and operations in over 125 countries) with many policies and procedures. Yet despite its size and policies there are always unique situations and new questions they have never heard. During my ten-year career, they have answered every question I have posed and considered every proposition I have suggested. The key is not being afraid to ask the question or propose an idea. When I got pregnant with Sarah, I spoke to a close friend and confidant at work about job sharing. At that point in the company's history (over 125 years) no one in "line" marketing (general-manager path with profit-and-loss responsibility) had job shared. In fact, very few had tried and been successful at any type of reduced work schedule. The job was simply too time consuming. It would have been easy to think we were just dreaming, but instead we went to the head of Global Marketing for our business unit and proposed our idea. Not surprising, they listened and were very interested. They asked us to put together a proposal and began to work to find the ideal pilot role. In the end we didn't job share, as my partner's situation changed, but it was refreshing to know the company's openness to piloting job sharing.

Like asking for help with your children, the key is simply to ask. If you need to work from home to provide some flexibility, then ask. If you need to limit travel to certain days of the week or month, ask for it. If you cannot move to another country or location due to family commitments, then let the company know. Most companies are thrilled to have strong female managers and want to work to help them balance their work and household situations. If your requests are reasonable and you do your homework before making them, I think you will be pleasantly surprised with the answers you get.

Tips and Time Savers:

For Managing Life

This section provides tips for all those other things you do in life that don't fit under children, you, your home, or your career. I had a really hard time figuring out what to call this section. I tried to force the tips into one of the other four areas, but they simply didn't fit there. Life is staying in touch with family and friends, your vacations, documenting life via photos, sending gifts to loved ones, entertaining, and more. It is what you do on a Saturday night, or the random errands you need to run over the weekend. When you have children, it is the hardest part to keep up with. It will become very easy to loose touch with friends, skip vacations, and never print those digital pictures. This section will provide you with a few tips to make "life" a bit easier.

MAKE FRIDAY NIGHT PIZZA NIGHT

After a long week at work, the last thing you want to do on Friday night is cook. You also don't want to be in a crowded restaurant with young children in your state of exhaustion. This is why I encourage you to make Friday night pizza night. This tip was given to me by Deb Henretta, who is now Group President of P&G's Asian operations. I went to a women's lunch and someone asked her how she managed it all, and she talked about how her family started a tradition of having pizza with their neighbors every Friday and how much the kids and parents loved it. We now do the same thing. At about 4 P.M. each Friday we call/instant message/e-mail around to our neighbors we're friendly with and ask them if they are in for pizza that night. We normally get at least one family to join us and rotate whose house we go to and who pays. This often turns into game night for the adults and a movie for the kids. The kids are happy because what's better than pizza and a video with their friends. The adults get to relax in good conversation and company. And all it takes is one click to order online or a phone call.

ALL-INCLUSIVE RESORT VACATIONS

This was a late discovery for our family, but what a find. Vacations are essential in a dual-career-with-kids household for many reasons; they provide needed R and R, valuable time with the children, and serve as a reward for all your hard work. With young children, vacations aren't always relaxing, rewarding, or fun. You worry about traveling, particularly on airplanes. You worry about where, what, and when you will eat. You want to spend time with the kids, but you would also like some alone time with your spouse. You worry about the cost of the vacation, because flying kids is as expensive as flying adults. Suddenly planning and taking a vacation becomes very stressful. The solution is an all-inclusive vacation where airfare, lodging, meals, and limited entertainment are included in the price.

The founding father of the all-inclusive vacation is the French company Club Med. Now various companies offer all-inclusive vacations throughout the world, from beach to ski vacations. We have taken vacations with three different all-inclusive companies: Apple Vacation, Vacations Express, and Club Med. We found all three to meet our needs perfectly, offering a beautiful surrounding with all the amenities we needed, specifically:

- Many food options, available throughout the entire day so we could eat whenever we needed

- Babysitting services available so we could leave Ben if we took a tour or saw an evening show

- Activities throughout the day from snorkeling, kayaking, swimming, aerobics, sailing, etc.

- Spa services on-site—a great getaway for mom or dad

- Transportation from the airport to the hotel and back

- Tours—they have companies offering various tours to experience the local culture and landscape, limiting the amount of research and planning needed on your part

In addition to supplying the basic services mentioned above, many also offer additional amenities for children. When you book the vacation be sure to contact the resort and ask if they have strollers and car seats for families to use while at the resort. This will save you the luggage and stress of carrying additional items with you.

Another type of all-inclusive vacation that we have found extremely family-friendly is a cruise. We have only taken one with kids, but we know plenty of friends who have done the Disney Cruise with young children. When Ben was eight months old we took a Princess cruise on the Baltic sea (Norway, Denmark, Sweden, Finland, Russia, Poland, and Estonia). We had dreamed about going to Stockholm, Helsinki, and St. Petersburg before we departed Europe, but didn't feel very comfortable doing this with a young baby. One day I got an e-mail from a Web site regarding discount cruises and found a Baltic cruise for $800 per person and Ben was free! With cruises the flights are not included to get to the disembarkation port. It was a perfect solution for us; the boat could be our transportation and provide the "safe haven" for lodging that we were looking for, and it was a fraction of what the trip would be had I planned it all.

This was an ideal solution. Like all-inclusive resorts, the food, lodging, and entertainment are included, and they have a spa, gym, and babysitting if needed. They even supplied us with baby food at our dinner table each evening. You can go onshore to tour as much or as little as you please. The buses were very child-friendly with ample storage for our stroller and gear. Best of all, we felt like Ben had one hundred pairs of grandparents onboard; everyone doted on him and gave him lots of love and attention.

Today there are lots of "child focused" cruise lines like Disney. I would encourage you to ask friends and do some online research to determine which you think would be best for your family.

EQUIP BOTH CARS WITH CAR SEATS

When both parents work outside the home, you never know what each day will bring you. It can be very smooth and you leave work as planned at your normal time, or one of you can have a late-day fire drill that requires immediate attention and keeps you later than you thought. The easiest way to manage unexpected changes in your schedule and still ensure the kids are picked up safe and sound is to have car seats in both of your cars. This allows either parent to pick up the children. We had friends who, like us, had three children in daycare, but they only had car seats in one car. This meant the parent who dropped off in the morning had to pick up. This often added a lot of stress for them, and did not allow any flexibility in schedule at the end of the day. It also means that if someone got sick and needed to be picked up and taken home, you would either have to take all the children home with you (which means you will get nothing done, like conference calls, etc., which could be taken from home), or drive back to daycare later to pick the other children up. It is a relatively small investment to have two of every size car seat—many used seats are for sale online or at consignment shops. This eliminates the need to juggle cars and let's you have more peace of mind should an emergency or change of plans arise.

ENTERTAINMENT FOR THE LONG CAR RIDES

We have found that since our third child was born, we drive more often than fly. Our trips to see my family in New York are no longer economical or simple since our third child. On top of the expense of the airfare, trying to transport five people once we get there can be expensive if you have to rent a car. If you are fortunate to have family that can lend you a car, this means you have to check car seats which also takes a lot of juggling and effort (like getting them out of your car). Taking all this into account, we have decided to drive on most of our trips that can be done in one day.

The downside to this is keeping your children happy for more than ten hours. Here are some things that we have found useful for these types of trips. The first is a DVD player in the car. With young children there typically isn't too much disagreement on the type of videos, so just bring an assortment, and you should be fine. We normally ask each child which video they want to watch ahead of time and make sure they get to watch at least one of their requests. The second tip comes from my neighbor Catherine. She suggested bringing TV tables/trays into the car to use for eating as well as coloring, drawing, and workbooks. I found great ones for the kids at K-mart that fit nicely over their car seats and have storage on both sides to hold crayons, markers, books, sippy cups, and more. The final tip is to eat at least one meal in the car, which is made easier by the tray tables. While we normally shy away from this, on long trips like this, once the kids are out of the car, it's difficult to coax them back into the car. To get around this we try to eat our lunch in the car and then take at least an hour to sit down to a nicer dinner to allow the kids to release some energy and for us to enjoy a more relaxing meal.

INTERNET SITES AND CHAT ROOMS

The great thing about the Internet is that it is very easy to find people like you—the same family situation, the same hobbies, or interests. When you have young children there are a variety of helpful sites online for you to browse and find answers to your questions. In Cincinnati we have one called cincymoms.com. It has chat rooms where you can post a question, and within hours, get answers from a diverse group of women. It is a great way to learn from other women based on their wisdom and past experiences rather than going at it alone. You can save quite a bit of time if you do the research ahead of time and ask the right experts.

To find the site that is right for you, do some searching with key words on Google, Yahoo, or another search engine. Spend some time browsing the various sites they recommend and see which ones feel like a fit for you. You can also ask other new moms in your neighborhood, at work, or another group to see which sites they find useful. I would recommend finding a local site if one exists, as you'll be able to find great information on local doctors, hospitals, children's activities, support groups, and more.

DIGITAL PHOTOS AND ONLINE PHOTO STORAGE

Children are such precious gifts that you will find you want to capture every key moment in their lives. You will also find that your family *expects* you to capture all of these moments, particularly if they live out of town, as this is their way of watching their grandchild, niece, or nephew grow. Digital cameras are one of the greatest inventions for a parent of a young child. You can now snap away like crazy trying to capture the first smile, first tooth, first pull-up, first birthday, and more. You simply delete the photos you don't want and upload all the rest. I recommend using an Internet photo site to store and purchase your photos. Here's why:

1. Your family and friends can log on to see your photos and purchase copies if they want.

2. They give you free storage space.

3. They have every type of service you need: printing, gift making, CD making, etc.

4. It serves as a backup in case your hard drive ever goes bad, and you haven't stored the photos on a CD.

Our family uses Snapfish.com, and we have been very happy with the service and value. I purchase prints in bulk, often 500 or 1,000 at a time and pay as low as ten cents a photo. I have also had calendars made, and my mother had a mug made—both of us were very satisfied with the end product. Shipping and handling is a bit high, so I try to ship them in bulk instead of every time I upload the photos. We have other family members and friends who use Shutterfly and Kodak and are also happy with the service. You are safe with any of the major sites. Browse each site and choose the one that feels comfortable to you with regards to navigation, as the prices are all very competitive.

When you send the photos out for viewing to friends take the time to send an e-mail update on your family and how you are all doing. This is a great way of staying in touch. Often it also produces response e-mails with updates on their family. In today's world where it is so hard to stay in touch, this is a great way to give your friends and family a glimpse into your life. ☺

E-CARDS AND CALENDAR SERVICES

By far the hardest thing I find to keep up with is birthdays, anniversaries, and other important occasions. I used to go to the card store and buy five to ten cards at a time, never missing a key date, but when the kids came and life was busier I discovered e-cards. While they are certainly not the same as a real card you send through the postal service, they still show you care and comunicate nice wishes to your loved one. More important, the large e-card sites have services where you can set up an online calendar with all your important dates. Once you input your names and dates, the site sends you a reminder a week in advance with a link to their site and e-cards. They have a variety of cards to choose from—simply pick one out, personalize it, and type in the date you want it sent. No more excuses for missing an important occasion. I have used hallmark.com, americangreetings.com, and bluemountain.com—all large e-card sites that have a large selection and reminder services. It will take a couple of hours to type in all the dates and e-mail addresses, but it is well worth it in the end. You'll save time, reduce stress, and put smiles on the faces of your friends and loved ones.

CATCH UP WITH FAMILY AND FRIENDS DURING DRIVE TIMES

We all spend more time in our car than we care to. While this can be great downtime to decompress from a hard day's work or prep for the day ahead, it can also be used to catch up with family and friends. I would recommend getting a good headset for your cell phone so you still have both hands free to drive. I have found having the headset is only half the battle: the other half is remembering to use it. ☺ As you drive to work or a meeting at another location, dial your mom, sister, or friend to catch up with them. Once you get home from work, you are so busy handling the kids, dinner, baths, and more that there simply isn't a quiet moment to call. When you do finally settle down for the night it is often too late to make the phone call. Be sure to have all your key numbers programmed in your cell phone, as calling information on cell phones is very costly, and you often don't have a pen and paper to write down the number if the call fails.

BRING A PACKED LUNCH OR DINNER WITH YOU

No matter how much you plan, you will have evening or weekend outings that happen during a normal meal time. For us these are Tuesday nights, when we have swim lessons, and some weekend afternoons. I have found it much easier to pack a lunch or dinner and bring it with me than try to find food at the location or eat dinner at a later time. Each Tuesday we have swim lessons that begin at 6:30 with Sarah's lesson followed by Ben and Claire's lesson at 7:00. By the time we bathe the children, we don't get home until 8:00 at the earliest. For the children, this is a bit late to eat, so that gives us two options—leave work even earlier (Arnie leaves by 5:00 to get the children and arrive on time), or feed them at the YMCA. Each Tuesday morning I pack a cooler with sippy cups, yogurt, fruit, salami, cheese and crackers, apple sauce, cheese sticks, and cookies for dessert. This gives the children enough variety to choose from while having a healthy, complete meal. Some other favorites of neighbors of ours are PB&J, other sandwiches, and granola bars.

We found this so easy and helpful that we began to do this on the weekends. If we decide to go to the zoo we bring a similar type of cooler with us. While there is plenty of food at the zoo it can be expensive and takes a lot of time to sit down. Bringing our own food saves us quite a bit of money and makes it easier, as we can feed the children in the stroller while we walk and view the animals instead of having to stop, unload everyone, find a table, order, and eat. Get to know what your children like and pack a meal. You will save quite a bit of stress, time, and money while giving yourself much more flexibility in your weekend and evening activities.

HOST ANNUAL PARTIES AT YOUR HOME

Once you have children it becomes very difficult to stay in touch with friends, particularly if they are having children at the same time as you are. The easiest way to be sure to see your friends at least a few times a year is to host annual gatherings at your home. Pick a time of year or type of event that you enjoy (such as the Superbowl, Final Four, Oscars, Halloween) and begin to make it a tradition. It becomes easier to host the event with each passing year, as you know what to make, how many people will be there, and have the invitation and other essentials done. The other great thing about this is you get to cook once but see a lot of your friends. The rule in our house is I never cook for less than six. If we are having a dinner party we have to invite at least two couples and their families to join us. If you are going to go through the effort, make it truly worthwhile by getting to spend quality time with a group of friends.

Each year we host the following events: a holiday brunch in December for about one hundred people; cake and coffee with the neighbors for Claire's birthday; an anniversary barbecue the weekend that we moved to our home in June; a barbecue for Ben and Sarah's birthdays; the neighborhood ladies' holiday cookie exchange; the P&G beauty women's taskforce holiday event; and dinners for both of our work groups. These events allow us to see all of our close friends, colleagues, and neighbors at least once a year, and allow us to entertain in our home where we find it easier to manage, and we never have to leave the kids.

CREATE LISTS FOR KEY PARTIES AND MAILINGS

Being a busy family should not stop you from entertaining and getting those Christmas cards out. But it does stop you from having all the time in the world to prepare and think about it. Take some time to get these events and mailings organized, and you will find you look forward to them rather than dreading that time of year. Create a folder that holds all the key information for each event. First, think about what annual events you have at your home, such as birthday parties, barbecues (Fourth of July, Memorial Day, Labor Day), holiday parties (Halloween, Christmas, New Years, Easter), and work parties. Once you have a folder created for each event, the following information should be included: 1) invitation list—with names and addresses, 2) last year's invitation list—including where the file is located on your computer, 3) menu—what you served, and how much of it.

This will make the planning much easier. I also like to have decorative paper in the house so I can easily make the invitations rather than having to run to the store to buy them. I also save time by buying a lot of easy-to-make food items at Sam's or Costco to keep it simple, casual, and fun. The most important thing is spending time with or connecting with friends and family, not the appetizers or decorations.

ENTERTAIN AT HOME

Many dual-career couples feel additional guilt when they go out without the children. For most, the majority of the workweek is spent away from the kids, and hence they try to limit the amount of time away from them during the weekends. On top of feeling some guilt about going out, it can be difficult to find a sitter, especially if you have decided on a whim. Our solution is to entertain at home. If your friends have kids they can bring them over and have them play with yours; if not, you can simply pop in a video and let your kids have a treat while you sit down for a nice dinner with friends. For larger dinner parties I recommend hiring a babysitter to come to the house. This allows your guests to relax and have a good time rather than worrying about their children. Also, if you have a sitter, it's much easier to have the kids play in the basement or play room and away from the dining room so you can enjoy a quiet conversation with friends. There will be times when one or all of your kids want to be with mom and dad and not with the other kids or their siblings. Let them sit on your lap while you have a nice conversation with friends. It's still better than having every conversation through e-mail!

ONLINE SHOPPING

The Internet is a wonderful tool, bringing stores, news, knowledge, and more to your fingertips each day. For a busy household it can be a godsend, particularly when it comes to shopping. Almost every major retailer has an online site allowing you to purchase goods without having to leave your home. When you live away from your family, this comes in very handy for sending gifts, saving you the trip to the post office. I have been using the Internet to purchase goods for over five years, because it saves me time but also usually saves me a lot of money. Here's why:

- The mall, travel agent, ticketmaster, and, in some areas, the grocery store are in your house rather than a drive away
- The sales are every day
- You have access to more products
- It does the price comparison for you (on sites like buy. com, shopzilla.com)
- You can do your research and purchase at the same time
- It does the shipping for you

I have been using the Internet to purchase travel, clothing, toys, cigars, furniture, and more. During this time I have never had a security issue or failed to have the goods delivered on time. In the same time I had a store credit-card number taken while in the store and used to purchase almost $1,000 in goods. The Internet is safe, fast, and often cheaper.

HAVE GIFTS ON HAND IN THE HOUSE

This is probably one of my biggest time-and-money saving tips. Once you have children you will find you need an incredible amount of gifts, particularly new baby and birthday gifts. You will transition from wedding gifts to baby gifts quicker than you can say "baby." For out-of-town gifts, I do a lot of my shopping online as I mentioned earlier. This is the quickest and simplest way to get the gift to the recipient in a timely fashion. As my kids have gotten older, I have found I buy more gifts in bulk and simply plan to go to the post office a couple times a month to mail them to friends instead of shopping online only. For local gifts I keep a stock of age-appropriate gifts in what we call our "gift armoire" (see photo). Here are things to remember when stocking up on gifts: 1) make sure you have gifts appropriate for both genders, 2) make sure you have gifts appropriate for all the ages of your children (as you will likely get invited to like-age birthdays), 3) get gift receipts for all purchases and tape them to gifts, 4) have new baby gifts appropriate for first, second, third, or fourth child, and 5) don't limit baby gifts to clothes, as it may be second girl or boy, and clothes are not necessary.

About twice a year I hit Toys R Us when they are having a big sale and stock up on items for the ages of my children. I try to stay very generic as opposed to choosing trendier gifts so they don't go out of style. For example, get fire trucks and construction vehicles for boys; Barbie, princess, or Dora items for girls. For younger infants and toddlers, Fisher Price is always a hit. I keep at least two infant boy and infant girl (six to twelve months) items on hand. I have the most luck at Sam's Club and Costco when it comes to clothes, as well as the Carter's and OshKosh outlets. I also keep a stock of what I call "third child" gifts, the gift to give when they don't need girl or boy clothes. My favorites are blankets, picture frames, or hand-foot print kits, which I find at the Pottery Barn outlet. Finally, I like to give little gifts to the siblings when a second or third child is born. My friend Megan O'Donnell was the first to do this for Ben when Claire was born, and boy did he just love it. From that point on I tried to remember to do the same. My favorite choice for this is soft hand puppets I found at Costco for $7.50 for four, or puzzles.

Gift armoire

SAVE DELIVERY BOXES TO MAKE POST OFFICE TRIPS EASY

Going to the post office is never an easy task. Typically on weekends there are long lines, and balancing your various boxes for shipping is always a nightmare. When you have to pack it up in the post office and address a label, it can become extremely time-consuming and stressful. I try to save any box I get—from large boxes received in shipments via UPS or FedEx to shoe boxes and everything in between. Whenever I have to ship something I go into my "box" closet, which is under our stairs, and find an appropriate size. I also save all the packing materials that come with shipments—bubble wrap, peanuts, and packing paper, so I have the necessary materials to pack it safe and sound. You should also buy packing tape to secure the box after the contents are packed. We buy ours in bulk at Sam's Club. Finally, take a piece of paper, or the card if you are sending one, and write the address on it, and secure it with the tape. This will make your post office trip as smooth as possible, and save you lots of money in boxes and packing materials.

GO FOR THE SIMPLER BIRTHDAY PARTIES

I am not sure how it started, but at around the age of three very large birthday parties have become the norm in our society. I can't tell you how many weekends we have spent at Kids First or Run, Jump, -n- Play, which are two Cincinnati-area birthday factories. While the kids have fun, there isn't too much fun in watching twenty or so kids run and scream for two hours, eat pizza, and open gifts in mad chaos. Arnie and I have tried to avoid this trend. Our children already have far too many toys in the house and we cherish our weekends for family time, not shuttling from party to party.

What we do instead is bring some sort of entertainment into daycare for their party. We share the expenses with another family whose two children happen to be born on the same day and one week prior to ours. This allows us to skip the gifts and doesn't require twenty families to rearrange their weekend plans for us. The kids absolutely love it, and you can try different things each year. So far we have done a magician, juggler/acrobat, and ballet dancer. The daycare also loves it as the children get exposed to different artists and crafts.

If you are not allowed to bring entertainment into your school and aren't ready for the big birthday factory or to host a party at your home, my friend Kristy gave me the tip of having a party at the firehouse. For a small donation you can have pizza and cake, get to slide down the pole, and even put on the hat for a photo with the truck. If you want to also escape the gifts simply tell the other parents "no gifts please" or that you will be donating the gifts to a local charity.

GIFT BAGS VERSUS WRAPPING GIFTS

Most of you who are reading this book probably already use this tip. If you don't, start today. Gift bags are a godsend to busy households, not only making life easier but also saving you money in the process. While it is nice to get a beautifully wrapped gift every now and then, á la Martha Stewart, what's really important is the thought that went into it, not the presentation. Here are my top five reasons to start using gift bags today:

1. They're so easy. Just throw in some tissue paper, the gift, and off you go—maybe one minute of work versus a good five to ten minutes for wrapping a gift.

2. They require no additional tools or products like scissors, tape, gift tag (they come with one).

3. They can be reused. I save all the bags we get and reuse them (as long as you don't "re-gift" what's inside!).

4. There is a wide variety of sizes and styles, more so than paper.

5. They're cheap. Try to find them in bulk if you can. My best finds were at Costco. First I found a set of twenty-five holiday bags for around $18, then on another trip I got twenty-one adorable all-occasion bags for the same amount, less than a dollar per bag. The sets ranged from very large to smaller more creative bags. The all-occasion set included birthday, baby, wedding, thank you, wine bag, etc.

Farewell

The Zucker family at Walt Disney World April 2006.
I returned to work exactly one week later. ☺

Sadly, I have come to the end of "my book." This was one of the most rewarding and, in many ways, freeing experiences in my life. I looked forward to the days when I had thirty minutes to sit down at my computer and write another tip. As I drafted my thoughts I would imagine I was talking to a friend, like you, who had asked for some honest advice on how I attempt to manage it all. I hope you found the book warm and personal. I hope you learned something and will continue to refer to the book to find ways to make your life a bit easier.

The tips in this book have helped Arnie and me enjoy a more peaceful life. I hope they will do the same for you. Enjoy every minute with your children, feel fulfilled at work, and have a home filled with love and happiness. I would love to hear some of your tips on how you manage it all. Please send them to me at joanna@ millenniummom.com. You can also blog with me at www.millen-niummom.com

Appendices

APPENDIX A—DAYS IN THE LIFE

As I thought about what Arnie and I do to make life a bit easier with young children, I started to write down what a typical day looked like. I also realized our days were different if I was on maternity leave or traveling, versus working in Cincinnati. On the following pages, I have outlined some of my typical days to help you get a sense of what a day in your future may look like, how I multitask throughout the day, where Arnie and I partner or divide and conquer and more. I hope you get some insights from our days, but I encourage you to go through this exercise to try to help you understand what your day looks like and how you can apply some of the tips from the book to help you save time, stress, or be more productive.

Maternity Leave #2, June 3, 2004

6:45 A.M.	Feed Claire
7:15	Dress Claire, lie in bed with her
7:30	Wash face, brush teeth, get dressed
7:45	Ben up, dress and sit with Ben
8:00	Ben brush teeth, take vitamin while Claire in swing
8:15	Breakfast for Ben and me, empty dishwasher while waiting for toast, pump to extract extra milk while eating
8:30	Clean up breakfast (Ben in high chair), put milk in refrigerator, Claire in car seat, pack car to bring Ben to daycare, call Mom from car
9:05	Drop Ben off
9:35	Back home, call Panasonic regarding broken DVD player, play with Claire, feed Claire while reading *US* magazine
10:25	Claire plays on Gymini mat, write thank-you notes
11:00	Lay Claire down to sleep, log on to personal e-mail, log on to work e-mail, work on my subordinates' work and development plans, send files to my assistant to print for me.
1:00 P.M.	Lunch for me, read *US* magazine
1:30	Claire awakes, change diaper and feed her
2:00	Take walk with Claire, buy milk at convenience store
3:00	Arrive home, sort mail, play with Claire, eat snack, take pictures and some video of Claire, watch *General Hospital*
3:45	Claire napping in swing
4:00	Make bed, take dinner ingredients out (pasta)
5:00	Feed Claire and change diaper
5:30	Claire in bouncy seat, fill in baby calendar and book

6:15	Go for another walk with Claire
6:50	Arnie and Ben arrive home, play outside
7:15	Start dinner, Arnie outside with kids
7:45	Eat dinner, Claire sleeping
8:15	Clean up with Arnie, play with and read to Ben
9:00	Arnie puts Ben to bed, pick up toys, watch baseball game, read work printouts sent home with Arnie
9:30	Feed Claire, change diaper, put pajamas on
10:30	Claire and I to bed

Maternity Leave #2, June 15, 2004

6:30 A.M.	Claire awakes and eats, change diaper, back to bed
7:15	Ben up, Arnie gets him ready for daycare and takes him
7:45	Get up, shower, dress, make bed, throw a load of laundry in, eat breakfast
8:15	Get Claire in car seat, go to Volvo for car service
8:45	Car will be quick, wait instead of getting loaner car, do makeup and feed Claire while waiting
9:45	Car finished, go home, extract milk, and dress Claire
10:15	Go to playgroup
12:00 P.M.	Feed Claire at playgroup, change diaper, and eat lunch
1:30	Leave playgroup, stop at Macy's department store to pick up Arnie's sport coat, shop for summer clothes
3:00	Arrive at daycare to pick up Ben, feed Claire in Cardinal room where she will go
4:00	Pick up Ben from Busy Bees, his daily tells me to bring in diapers and wipes
4:15	Stop at Bigg's supermarket to pick up veggies, fruit, meat, juice, diapers, and wipes
5:15	Arrive home, put groceries away, prep dinner (marinate chicken, cut veggies)
5:30	Video in for Ben, play with kids, go through mail
6:00	Feed Claire, change diaper, play with Ben (sing songs)
6:45	Arnie arrives home, takes kids to play while I extract milk, start dinner
7:30	Eat dinner
8:00	Claire to sleep, play with Ben, watch Reds game, Arnie folds clothes

9:00	Arnie puts Ben to bed, Pistons game on TV, read *US* while Claire naps on me
10:00	Feed Claire and change diaper
10:30	Claire to bed, watch game with Arnie
11:30	Go to bed
3:30 A.M.	Claire up for feeding

Back to work, April 21, 2006

5:15 A.M.	Arnie wakes up and heads to YMCA
6:45	Joanna wakes up, washes face, brushes teeth, does hair and makeup
	Arnie returns to house
6:50	Arnie prepares grapes and strawberries for kids to take in car, puts briefcase in car
7:00	Joanna gets dressed and heads to Sarah's room to breast-feed
	Arnie wakes Ben up and gets him dressed
7:10	Arnie wakes Claire up and gets her dressed
7:15	Joanna dresses Sarah
	Arnie gives Ben and Claire vitamins, brushes their teeth and combs hair
	Ben and Claire come in to see Sarah, Arnie makes bed
7:20	Everyone heads downstairs
	Coats and shoes on
	Breakfast bowls and juice cups given to kids
	Joanna searches for Pooh stuffed animal for Claire to take to school
	Joanna gives "pick up" bag to Arnie for blankets and bottles (it's Friday)
7:30	Buckle everyone in
7:36	We pull out of driveway, both cars together
8:02	Arrive at daycare, sign in
8:05	Drop Claire off and fill out paperwork
8:12	Drop Ben off and fill out paperwork
8:20	Drop off Sarah, fill out paperwork, talk to teachers about her eating and how she is doing (it's her first week), drop off bottles
8:32	Pull into P&G garage and begin work day

2:30 P.M.	Joanna leaves work for 3:00 appointment
4:00	Pump while waiting at appointment
5:15	Arnie leaves work (yeah, it's Friday, a bit early)
5:30	Joanna done with appointment and heads home, Arnie arrives at daycare, picks Sarah up
5:40	Arnie picks Ben up
5:45	Arnie picks Claire up, Joanna arrives home
5:50	Arnie and kids head home
6:00	Joanna begins dinner
6:10	Joanna goes through mail and pulls out bills to pay over weekend
6:20	Arnie and kids arrive home, Joanna takes blankets upstairs for wash
6:40	Feed Sarah her food
6:45	Rest of family eats dinner
7:15	Clean up from dinner
7:30	Head outside to let kids play with neighbors
8:40	Arrive back home
8:50	PJs on, read books
	Joanna breast-feeds Sarah, Sarah to bed
9:15	Claire and Ben to bed
	Joanna and Arnie chat, plan out weekend, watch TV
	Joanna puts together gift bags for friend's new adopted twins who they will meet on Sunday
10:00	Joanna to bed
11:30	Arnie to bed

Weekend in the Life—Saturday April 22, 2006

7:30 A.M.	Ben and Claire come into our room and bed
	Arnie up, Joanna trying to wake up
7:40	Ben and Claire go into sitting room to watch Playhouse Disney
7:45	Arnie gets Sarah and brings her to bed, Joanna breast-feeds
	Arnie brings bowls of grapes and juice cups up to Ben and Claire
	Arnie departs for bike ride
8:00	Sarah joins Ben and Claire for *Little Einstein*, Joanna gets dressed and begins to gather laundry
8:15	Joanna folds two loads from last night, throws another load in
8:45	Claire on potty (getting trained)
9:00	Back to laundry, make bed, prep "drop off" bag for Monday (spare clothes, blankets, etc.) and put it in car
9:15	Feed Sarah breakfast, empty dishwasher
9:30	Continue laundry, change Sarah's diaper, dress Sarah and put her clothes away
9:45	Arnie back home, dress Ben while Arnie showers, put Ben's clothes away, lay out clothes for the week
10:00	Dress Claire, put Claire's clothes away, and lay out clothes for the week
10:15	Sarah down for nap, Joanna showers
10:30	Arnie and Joanna eat
11:00	Everyone downstairs to wait for photographer to arrive
	Clean up kitchen, pick up toys lying around, and comb kids' hair
11:15	Photographer arrives, Sarah up, take family photo

12:00 P.M.	End of photos, Arnie and I go upstairs to change clothes, change Sarah's diaper and clothes, fix lunch for everyone (yogurt, cheese sticks, and turkey for kids), throw anther load of laundry in
12:30	Clean up lunch, Arnie outside to mow lawn, Joanna and kids outside to play
1:00	Blow up bouncy house on lawn and have neighbors' kids over
1:15	Breast-feed Sarah
1:30	Sarah down for nap, kids play outside, another load of laundry
2:00	Sarah wakes up
2:30	Send neighbors home, put shoes on kids, Claire and Ben on potty, load kids in car
2:45	Depart for haircut, kids fall asleep in car
3:00	Joanna hair appointment, Arnie stays in car with kids
4:00	Joanna done, drive to Sam's Club (kids still sleeping)
4:15	Arrive Sam's, kids wake up, go shopping
5:35	Checkout, Joanna breast-feeds Sarah, order pizza to go
6:00	Arrive home, unload groceries, change everyone's clothes (ice-pop demo leaked all over everyone), another load of laundry
6:20	Eat pizza for dinner
6:30	Clean up, go outside to play, kids on swing set, Joanna builds fire in firepit
7:15	Walk to neighbors' house to let kids play
8:30	Breast-feed Sarah (while sitting on blanket on neighbors' lawn)
8:45	Walk home
9:00	Joanna and Sarah sit outside watching fire, Ben and Claire inside watching video

9:15	Sarah falls asleep, put in crib
9:30	Joanna works on book while sitting on patio, Arnie puts Claire and Ben to sleep
10:00	Joanna upstairs, folds three loads of laundry and puts way
10:20	Joanna to bed, Arnie watching TV

Sunday April 23, 2006

8:00 A.M.	Arnie and Joanna begin to stir in bed
8:10	Sarah cooing in her crib, Arnie goes to get her
8:15	Breast-feed Sarah in bed, Arnie gets Claire
8:20	Ben crying (his pull-up leaked all over bed), get Ben and strip his clothes and sheets, prepare a bath
8:30	Arnie bathes Ben and Claire, Joanna puts sheets in washer, Sarah sitting on bathroom floor, Joanna gets clothes for the day
8:40	Joanna washes face, brushes teeth, etc., Claire and Ben out of bath and dressed, Ben and Claire watch *Dora* (from DVR), Arnie gives Sarah bath
8:50	Joanna strips sheets from her bed, brings jackets downstairs and grabs new bag of Claire's pull-ups from garage
9:00	Sarah out of bath and dressed, Joanna gets dressed, Arnie gets dressed
9:15	Family downstairs for breakfast (bagels, frozen waffles, juice)
9:45	Joanna and Sarah head to church, Arnie cleans up breakfast, Ben and Claire play, Arnie throws in load of laundry
10:00	Potty break for Ben and Claire, Arnie outside with Ben and Claire to play
11:15	Church ends, Joanna and Sarah to grocery store, Sarah naps
11:45	Head home, unload groceries, empty kitchen garbage, refill snack bins in two cars, Ben and Claire on swings with Arnie
12:15 P.M.	Joanna cleans kitchen, sorts through mail, finishes dividing bulk goods bought at Sam's on Saturday, makes lunch for kids (clementine, yogurt, juice), makes cup of tea and reads paper

1:00	Joanna heads upstairs to fold laundry, make Claire's bed, take out clothes for Monday. Back downstairs to unload dishwasher and load in lunch dishes.
	Arnie outside with Ben and Claire, kids playing in yard, Arnie cleans gas grill
1:30	Sarah wakes up, feed her lunch
1:45	Joanna takes kids for a walk (Sarah in Baby Björn, Claire on push tricycle, Ben on his tricycle). Arnie spackles Sarah's wall, hangs some shelves and pictures
2:30	Return from walk, kids play inside, Joanna helps Arnie finish hanging items
2:45	Brandon (a neighbor) comes over to play with Ben, Jo and Arnie start preparing for company, get food ready, plates/bowls/cups/utensils, clean outside furniture
3:15	Breast-feed Sarah, put her in swing in yard, she falls asleep for a nap, Ben, Claire and Brandon have snack (cheese sticks)
4:15	Arnie takes Brandon home
5:00	The Molloys arrive for barbecue
	Kids play (seven kids between ages two and seven) outside while adults cook food and chat
	Eat around 6:45, breast-feed Sarah
8:15	Molloys depart, finish cleaning up
8:45	Upstairs for baths
9:15	Finish baths, get dressed, read books, breast-feed Sarah
9:30	Kids to bed
10:00	Arnie and Joanna in sitting room watching TV, talk about week to come
10:30	Joanna to bed, Arnie to office for some work

APPENDIX B—My top ten helpful things for your home

If money were no object, here are the ten things I would recommend to you when it comes to choosing a home or key upgrades to your home. They will save you stress, time, or energy, all things we could use to save.

1. **Extra garage**—If you need one, get two. If you need two, get three. You will always need the space and envy those who have it.

2. **Closet space**—As I said, I would trade an extra bedroom for closets any day. The key to getting organized is having a place for everything, and you need closets to achieve that.

3. **Pantry**—If you want to stock up to save time, you need some place to put it. I love my big pantry and would recommend it to anyone.

4. **Laundry room upstairs**—This is a new design theme in many new homes. We moved ours upstairs in the last year, and I love it—no more going up and down stairs with a heavy basket full of clothes. It saves time and energy.

5. **Hot water dispenser**—This was in our house when we moved in and it is awesome. You can warm up a bottle or defrost breast milk in no time. Have a cup of hot tea in seconds, and boiling water for pasta no longer takes half an hour.

6. **Mudroom**—Putting lockers into our mudroom was a godsend. All the coats, shoes, hats, gloves, and more are in one place, and I know where to find them. It also serves as the mail center. We get more junk mail than I know what

to do with, but at least I have a space to put it before I have time to sort through all of it.

7. **Wireless Internet connection**—When you do need to log on from home, this saves so much time and allows you to be close to your children at the same time. ☺

8. **Great room**—I love having the ability to make dinner and see my children at the same time. Even if it isn't the same room, having a family room attached to the kitchen is a great start.

9. **Hard floors versus carpet**—Children will get sick and spill many things in life. Rather than worry about the carpet staining I would recommend putting as many hard floors in your home as possible; hardwood, laminate, or tile are all good surfaces that are easy to clean and maintain.

10. **Leather or microfiber furniture**—These are easy-to-clean fabrics for the high-traffic areas in your home, like the kitchen and family room.

APPENDIX C—Ten things you can never have enough of for the kids

1. **Spit-up clothes**—No matter how many you have, they never seem to be where you need them. At least having more helps improve your odds.

2. **Pacifiers**—Like the disappearing socks, these things can hide better than anything else I know of.

3. **Diaper bags**—I like to keep one in each car, one stocked in the house to give to grandparents or sitters, and one smaller-sized one to stick in the carriage for walks.

4. **Blankets**—The perfect gift for a second or third baby. Every child needs them and often become attached to them. We need to send them into daycare each week for naps, so it's always good to have a bunch.

5. **Diaper-changing stations**—Have multiple locations in your home—why have to walk upstairs or down to change the diaper?

6. **Books**—The best thing you can do for your children is read to them often. We keep books everywhere in the house to encourage this: family room, playroom, bedrooms, basement, car, etc.

7. **Five-minute meals**—Anything that can be made in less than five minutes: Budget Gourmet pastas, hot dogs, cheese sticks, sandwich meat, tuna fish, PB&J, soup. Great things to leave with sitters for them to make for kids.

8. **Pretreater**—Keep a stick in your diaper bag or purse,

one on the hamper, and, of course, the laundry room. The commercials don't lie; kids seem to find every type of stain possible. ☺

9. **Balls**—As Barney says, "It's the greatest toy of all." Children learn so much coordination from kicking, throwing, hitting, or catching a ball. You can never have enough. Get soft ones for inside to limit potential damage.

10. **Hugs and Kisses**—The more the merrier in our household. It teaches kids how to demonstrate their feelings while making you feel like a million bucks when you receive one.

APPENDIX D—Household Tasks List

	Arnie	Joanna	Either*	Outsource
Cooking				
Breakfast			x	
Lunch			X	
Dinner			X	
Dishes/clear table			X — whoever doesn't cook	
Clean House		light cleaning	X	
Mow Lawn	X			
Lawn Maintenance				X — fertilizer
Laundry			X	
Bathe Children	X			
Grocery Shopping		X (or family)		
Clothes Shopping		X		
Painting		X		
House Misc. Tasks	X			
Pay Bills		X		
Sort Mail		X		
Book Appointments (doctors, car service, haircuts)		X		
Plan Vacations		X		
Investments	X			
Gift Giving		X		
Plan Social Events and Hire Sitter		X		

*Either = alternating nights, whoever has a free hand, or as needed

BLANK—Household Tasks List for You to Use

Either*   Outsource

Cooking
> Breakfast
> Lunch
> Dinner
> Dishes/clear table

Clean House

Mow Lawn

Lawn Maintenance

Laundry

Bathe Children

Grocery Shopping

Clothes Shopping

Painting
House Misc. Tasks

Pay Bills

Sort Mail

Book Appointments
  (doctors, car service, haircuts)

Plan Vacations

Investments

Gift Giving

Plan Social Events and Hire Sitter

> *Either = alternating nights, whoever has a free hand,
> or as needed

Appendix E: Easy Dinners (with Ingredients) for a Few Weeks

1. Barbecue (chicken, steak, sausage, burgers), fresh veggie (corn is great in summer), pasta side.

2. Chili (1 lb. meat, 1 chili season packet, large can diced tomatoes, 1 can kidney beans), rice.

3. Chicken parmagian (Italian-style chicken breasts from Sam's), spaghetti, mozzarella…place cooked chicken over pasta, add sauce and cheese, bake in oven to melt cheese.

4. Slow Cooker Helper (many varieties to choose from) with chicken or stew meat.

5. Supper Bakes (5+ varieties) simply add your chicken breast, comes with rice or pasta.

6. Soup and sandwiches, grilled cheese is great for rainy days, can also make paninis.

7. Lasagna—frozen from Sam's/Costco feeds a family and is done in microwave in 25 minutes.

8. Pasta—choose any variety (ziti, penne, farfelle, elbows are easier for kids) with a Classico sauce gives you great variety of taste.

9. Meatloaf (I like to make ahead on a weekend)— ground beef, bread crumbs, eggs, water, salt and pepper, ketchup, mustard, fresh veggie, Ore-Ida or Betty Crocker potato dish. Can substitute Stouffer's frozen meatloaf for homemade (saves a lot of time). If homemade, make more than one loaf and freeze.

10. Tacos—the kids love 'um, you can make a salad for yourself.

11. Quesadillas—soft tortilla, Kraft Mexican shredded cheese, mixture of veggies, chicken/beef/pork, sour cream, and salsa.

12. Pork chops—baked in oven with sauerkraut, fresh veggie, and Ore-Ida or Betty Crocker potatoes.

13. Sausage and pepper sandwiches—boil sausage to cook then grill either in skillet or gas grill, fry onions and peppers in olive oil. Serve sandwich style on Italian or French bread.

14. Baked ziti—cook ziti, mix in aluminum baking pan with marinara sauce (from jar is fine), riccotta cheese, parmesan cheese, and then sprinkle mozzarella on top. Bake in oven.

15. Frozen pizza—great for when your spouse is traveling, kids love it, and doesn't require any of your personal attention to cook.

16. Stouffer's frozen stuffed peppers, salad, and bread.

17. Breakfast for dinner—omelettes, pancakes, or French toast with bacon, OJ.

18. Baked salmon with a mustard/bread-crumb crust, fresh veggie, couscous (from box).

19. Chef's salad—cut up lunch meat and cheese onto lettuce, serve with bread.

20. Turkey steaks—(Sam's Club, wrapped in bacon), fresh veggie and pasta or rice side.

21. Meatball sandwiches—(can buy pre-made at Sam's or grocery store) on fresh Italian bread with a salad.

22. Mandarin chicken (Costco) served over rice with fresh steamed broccoli.

23. Grilled cheese sandwiches and soup.

24. Quiche (use Pillsbury pre-made crust)—eggs, vegetables, grated cheese.

25. Stew (in crock pot)—1 lb. stew meat, 4 large potatoes cubed, carrots, onions, flour, and water.

26. Pasta with beans—sauté garlic, onions, olive oil, and Italian herbs in large pot. Pour in 2 cans of kidney beans (substitute peas if you don't like beans). Add about 10 cups of water (same amount as you would to boil pasta; then pour in 1 lb. pasta. Bring to boil, then lower heat and simmer until almost all water is evaporated (about 40 minutes total).

27. Skillet Sensations or Bertolli frozen meals with Texas Toast.

Appendix F: Family Medical Leave Act and Pregnancy Discrimination Act

<u>Family Medical Leave Act (FMLA)</u> Synopsis of the Law

Covered employers must grant an eligible employee up to a total of twelve workweeks of unpaid leave during an twelve-month period for one or more of the following reasons:

- for the birth and care of the newborn child of the employee;
- for placement with the employee of a son or daughter for adoption or foster care;
- to care for an immediate family member (spouse, child, or parent) with a serious health condition; or
- to take medical leave when the employee is unable to work because of a serious health condition.

Pregnancy Discrimination Act (PDA)

The PDA is an amendment to Title VII of the Civil Rights Act of 1964. Discrimination on the basis of pregnancy, childbirth or related medical conditions constitutes unlawful sex discrimination under Title VII. Women affected by pregnancy or related conditions must be treated in the same manner as other applicants or employees with similar abilities or limitations.

<u>Hiring</u>—An employer cannot refuse to hire a women because of her pregnancy-related condition as long as she is able to perform the major functions of her job. An employer cannot refuse to hire her because of its prejudices against pregnant workers or the prejudices of co-workers, clients or customers.

<u>Pregnancy and Maternity Leave</u>—An employer may not single out pregnancy-related conditions for special procedures to deter-

mine an employee's ability to work. However, an employer may not use any procedure used to screen other employees' ability to work. For example, if an employer requires its employees to submit a doctor's statement concerning their inability to work before granting leave or paying sick benefits, the employer may require employees affected by pregnancy-related conditions to submit such statements.

If an employee is temporarily unable to perform her job due to pregnancy, the employer must treat her the same as any other temporarily disabled employee; for example, by providing modified tasks, alternative assignments, disability leave or leave without pay. Pregnant employees must be permitted to work as long as they are able to perform their job. If an employee has been absent from work as a result of a pregnancy-related condition and recovers, her employer may not require her to remain on leave until the baby's birth. An employer may not have a rule which prohibits an employee from returning to work for a predetermined length of time after childbirth. Employers must hold open a job for a pregnancy-related absence the same length of time jobs are held open for employees on sick or disability leave.

Health Insurance—Any health insurance provided by an employer must cover expenses for pregnancy-related conditions on the same basis as costs for other medical conditions. Health insurance for expenses arising from abortion is not required, except where the life of the mother is endangered. Pregnancy-related expenses should be reimbursed exactly as those incurred for other medical conditions, whether payment is on a fixed basis or a percentage of reasonable and customary charge basis. The amounts payable by the insurance provider can be limited only to the same extent as costs for other conditions. No additional, increased or larger deductible can be imposed. Employers must provide the same level of health benefits for spouses of male employees as they do for spouses of female employees.

Fringe Benefits—Pregnancy-related benefits cannot be limited to married employees. In an all-female workforce or job classification, benefits must be provided for pregnancy-related conditions if benefits are provided for other medical conditions. If an employer provides any benefits to workers on leave, the employer must provide the same benefits for those on leave for pregnancy-related conditions. Employees with pregnancy-related disabilities must be treated the same as other temporarily disabled employees for accrual and crediting of seniority, vacation calculation, pay increases and temporary disability benefits.

Taken from The U.S. Department of Labor and Equal Employment Opportunity Commission Web sites.

Easy Reference Tear Out

Quick Meals

Soup and Sandwiches

Grill a Meat, Veggie, Pasta Side

Breakfast for Dinner

Frozen Pizza

Pasta with Sauce and Bread

Frozen Lasagna

Chicken Parmagian

Chicken Helper

Chili and Rice

Skillet Sensations

Stouffer's Frozen Stuffed Peppers with Salad

Stouffers Meatloaf, Ore-Ida Potato and Veggie

Quesadillas

Tacos or Taco Salad

Chef Salad

Baked Ziti

Pork Chops, Couscous, and Veggie

Baked Salmon, Veggie, and Rice

Crock-Pot Stew

Lipton/Knorr Pasta Sides

Convenient Foods

Lipton/Knorr Rice Sides

Ore-Ida frozen potatoes

Stouffer's Frozen stuffed Peppers

Stouffer's Frozen Meatloaf

Betty Crocker Potatoes

Stouffers Skillet Sensations

Slow Cooker Helper

Campbell's Supper Bakes

Frozen Meatballs

Frozen Potstickers

Chunky and Progresso soups

Michelina's Budget Gourmet

Tear this page out to use as an easy reference.

Easy Reference Tear Out

Biggest Stress Savers

Lay clothes out the night before

Shower at night

All-inclusive vacations

Taking the day after vacation off

Coordinating calendars with husband

Hallmark.com

My BlackBerry

Being organized

Lists for everything

Being flexible

Following my gut

Asking for help

Snacks in the car

DVR and OnDemand TV for kids

Babysitter thirty minutes early

Set clear expectations at work

Biggest Time Savers

Online shopping

Gifts on hand

Multiple hampers

Hot water dispenser

Dirty clothes suitcase

Diaper stations around the house

Gift bags

Stocking up on household products

Easy-to-cook meals

Buy clothes ahead

Never walk upstairs empty handed

Lay clothes out the night before

Shipping materials on hand

Tear this page out to use as an easy reference.

Index

About the Author

Growing up in a working-class family taught Joanna Prokosch Zucker a strong work ethic and solid family values, which she now applies to her life as a full-time mom and business woman.

Joanna received a Bachelor degree of Science in Marketing, from the University of Scranton and while working on her MBA at the University of Michigan, interned at Proter & Gamble. She returned to work at Procter & Gamble fulltime, and there she met Arnie Zucker, and they were married in 2000. Together they have three children, Benjamin John, Claire Addison, and Sarah Loren.

Joanna was so often asked by her family, friends, and colleagues, "How do you do it?" that she began to track what she and Arnie did to make ends meet, manage the chaos of a dual-career family, and stay happy. In sharing her ideas and concepts with her peers and mentors, they encouraged her to pass on her experiences to others. On her third maternity leave with daughter Sarah, she wrote the book, *Millennium Mom*.

Joanna's hope is that *Millennium Mom* will save women a few minutes each day so they can feel less stressed, more fulfilled, and can enjoy life with their families as she doe s with her own family. You can email Joanna at joanna@millenniummom.com or you can blog with Joanna at www.millenniummom.com.